TEN BRITISH PICTURES

TEN
BRITISH
PICTURES

1740-1840

BY ROBERT R. WARK

THE HUNTINGTON LIBRARY · SAN MARINO

1971

FOR K.S.W.

Preface

THIS BOOK WAS WRITTEN with two objectives in mind. The first is to present a series of brief essays on several important and popular British paintings in the Huntington collection. From this point of view each chapter is a reasonably self-contained account giving information for a fuller understanding and enjoyment of a particular work.

The second objective of the book is to suggest, in terms of the ten pictures discussed, something of the scope and character of British painting of the Georgian period. The works all lie within a span of one hundred years, from the late 1730's to the late 1830's. The period is with little doubt the most brilliant in the history of British painting, but not necessarily the best understood. Naturally a book of this sort is not the place in which to attempt a full exploration of this highly complex phase of art history, but many of the salient characteristics are present in the pictures discussed.

The essays have taken shape over fifteen years. Several of them began as talks to the Friends of the Huntington Library; chapters III, IV, and V have appeared in slightly different form as independent pamphlets. Many professional colleagues, especially in England, have given me the benefit of their knowledge on special topics, and I am happy to have this opportunity to express my gratitude, if only in general terms. I am especially indebted to John Hayes, of the London Museum, Michael Kitson, of the Courtauld Institute, and Ronald Paulson, of The Johns Hopkins University, who read all or substantial parts of the manuscript of this book in close to its present form. Their criticisms and suggestions have been of the greatest value, although I should admit frankly that these scholars are not always in agreement with the ideas presented in the Introduction and various chapters. I am also grateful to Evelyn Joll and John Harris for generous assistance in the tedious business of tracking down photographs for the illustrations. The following individuals and institutions have graciously permitted the reproduction of works of art in their possession: Queen Elizabeth II; the Duke of Northumberland; Lady Oakes; Mr. Paul Mellon; Mrs. Flora Whitney Miller; Mr. Kurt F. Pantzer; Mrs. H. Scudamore; Art Institute of Chicago; British Museum; Cincinnati Art Museum; Coram Foundation for

Children; Graves Art Gallery, Sheffield; Lady Lever Art Gallery, Port Sunlight; Los Angeles County Museum of Art; National Gallery of Ireland; The National Gallery, London; The National Gallery of Victoria, Melbourne; The National Portrait Gallery, London; Royal Holloway College; Temple Newsam, Leeds; Trustees of the Petworth Estate; University of California at Los Angeles; Victoria and Albert Museum; The Wallace Collection.

ROBERT WARK

October, 1970

Contents

Chapter I. The Revolution in Eighteenth Century Art   3

Chapter II. Hogarth's "Bishop Hoadly"   15

Chapter III. Gainsborough's "The Blue Boy"   29

Chapter IV. Reynolds' "Mrs. Siddons as the Tragic Muse"   43

Chapter V. Lawrence's "Pinkie"   59

Chapter VI. Rowlandson's "Mrs. Siddons Rehearsing"   67

Chapter VII. Blake's "Satan, Sin, and Death"   79

Chapter VIII. Wilson's "River Scene with Bathers"   93

Chapter IX. Gainsborough's "The Cottage Door"   101

Chapter X. Constable's "View on the Stour near Dedham"   111

Chapter XI. Turner's "Grand Canal, Venice"   123

Illustrations

Unless otherwise noted, all works of art illustrated are from the Huntington collection.

Figure 1. François Boucher, *The Luncheon,* from *The Noble Pastoral,* designed in 1756, woven at the Beauvais tapestry works, 10 ft. 10 ins. x 11 ft.

Figure 2. J. Schmitz, *Chest,* French, mid-eighteenth century.

Figure 3. Henry Fuseli, *Johann Jakob Bodmer,* pencil, 17⅞ x 12½ ins.

Figure 4. Peter Romney, *Sophia Brierley,* brown and blue wash, 10¾ x 7¾ ins.

Figure 5. William Pars, *View of Rome,* watercolor, 18⅞ x 28¾ ins.

Figure 6. Thomas Gainsborough, *Boats on a Lake,* grey wash heightened with white, 11⅞ x 15-13/16 ins.

Figure 7. James Wyatt, *Design for Bowden,* from George Richardson, *The New Vitruvius Britannicus* (London 1802).

Figure 8. James Wyatt, *Fonthill Abbey,* from John Rutter, *Delineations of Fonthill and its abbey* (London 1823).

Figure 9. Robert Adam, *Entrance Hall at Syon House* (photo courtesy *Country Life*).

Figure 10. Robert Adam, *Ante-room at Syon House* (photo courtesy *Country Life*).

Figure 11. Robert Adam, *Drawing Room at Syon House* (photo courtesy *Country Life*).

Figure 12. Robert Adam, *Long Gallery at Syon House* (photo courtesy *Country Life*).

Figure 13. William Hogarth, *Bishop Benjamin Hoadly,* canvas, 24 x 19 ins.

Figure 14. Francis Hayman, *The Gascoigne Family,* canvas, 40 x 50 ins.

Figure 15. Arthur Devis, *Lord Lyttleton, his brother and sister-in-law,* canvas, 49½ x 39½ ins.

Figure 16. William Hogarth, *Mrs. Hoadly,* canvas, 24 x 19 ins.

Figure 17. William Hogarth, *Captain Coram,* canvas, 94 x 58 ins. (Thomas Coram Foundation for Children, London).

Figure 18. William Hogarth, *Marriage à la Mode, Scene I,* canvas, 27 x 35 ins. (The National Gallery, London).

Figure 19. William Hogarth, *Marriage à la Mode, Scene II,* canvas, 27 x 35 ins. (The National Gallery, London).

Figure 20. William Hogarth, *Marriage à la Mode, Scene III,* canvas, 27 x 35 ins. (The National Gallery, London).

Figure 21. William Hogarth, *Marriage à la Mode, Scene IV,* canvas, 27 x 35 ins. (The National Gallery, London).

Figure 22. William Hogarth, *Marriage à la Mode, Scene V,* canvas, 27 x 35 ins. (The National Gallery, London).

Figure 23. William Hogarth, *Marriage à la Mode, Scene VI*, canvas, 27 x 35 ins. (The National Gallery, London).

Figure 24. William Hogarth, *Bishop Benjamin Hoadly*, canvas, 49½ x 39½ ins. (The Tate Gallery, London).

Figure 25. B. Baron, after Hogarth, *Bishop Benjamin Hoadly*, engraving.

Figure 26. Thomas Gainsborough, *The Blue Boy*, canvas, 70 x 48 ins.

Figure 27. Thomas Gainsborough, *Lady with a Spaniel*, canvas, 30 x 25 ins.

Figure 28. Thomas Gainsborough, *Lady Petre*, canvas, 88¾ x 57¼ ins.

Figure 29. Sir Anthony Van Dyck, *George and Francis Villiers*, canvas, 54 x 50¼ ins. (H. M. Queen Elizabeth II).

Figure 30. Thomas Gainsborough, *Hon. Edward Bouverie*, canvas, 29½ x 24½ ins. (private collection, England).

Figure 31. Thomas Gainsborough, *The Blue Boy*, (detail).

Figure 32. Thomas Gainsborough, *The Blue Boy*, (x-ray detail).

Figure 33. Sir Joshua Reynolds, *Mrs. Siddons as the Tragic Muse*, canvas, 93 x 57½ ins.

Figure 34. Michelangelo, *Jeremiah*, from the Sistine ceiling, fresco (Anderson Art Reference Bureau).

Figure 35. Michelangelo, *Isaiah*, from the Sistine ceiling, fresco (Anderson Art Reference Bureau).

Figures 36 and *37*. Charles LeBrun, *Compassion* and *Fright*, from *Method to Learn to Design the Passions*, trans. John Williams (London 1734).

Figure 38. Cesare Ripa, *Melpomene*, from *Iconologia*, trans. George Richardson (London 1779).

Figure 39. Sir Joshua Reynolds, *Lavinia, Countess Spencer and Viscount Althorp*, canvas, 57½ x 43 ins.

Figure 40. Sir Joshua Reynolds, *Countess of Albemarle*, canvas, 49¾ x 39¾ ins. (The National Gallery, London).

Figure 41. Sir Joshua Reynolds, *Duchess of Hamilton*, canvas, 93 x 57 ins. (The Lady Lever Gallery, Port Sunlight).

Figure 42. Francis Haward, after Reynolds, *Mrs. Siddons as the Tragic Muse*, (detail, showing form of the signature on the hem of the dress), stipple engraving.

Figure 43. Sir Thomas Lawrence, *Pinkie*, canvas, 57½ x 39¼ ins.

Figure 44. Sir Thomas Lawrence, *Pinkie*, (detail).

Figure 45. Sir Thomas Lawrence, *Pinkie*, (detail).

Figure 46. Sir Thomas Lawrence, *Warren Hastings*, canvas, 35½ x 27½ ins. (The National Portrait Gallery, London).

Figure 47. Sir Thomas Lawrence, Countess of Blessington, canvas, 35 x 27¾ ins. (The Wallace Collection, London).

Figure 48. Thomas Rowlandson, *Mrs. Siddons Rehearsing*, pen and watercolor, 12¼ x 9 ins.

Figure 49. Thomas Patch, *Spencer Draper*, etching.

Figure 50. Thomas Rowlandson, *The Dissection*, pen, 14 x 19 ins.

Figure 51. Paul Sandby, *The Band Box Carrier*, pen and watercolor, 7⅞ x 6¼ ins.

Figure 52. Louis-Philippe Boitard, *Man Asleep*, pen and watercolor, 6⅞ x 5⅛ ins.

Figure 53. Charles Brandoin, *The Royal Academy Exhibition, 1771,* watercolor, 9-5/16 x 13$\frac{3}{4}$ ins.
Figure 54. Thomas Rowlandson, *Tailpiece,* from *Tour in a Post Chaise,* pen and watercolor, 4$\frac{1}{2}$ x 7-5/16 ins.
Figure 55. Thomas Rowlandson, *Delay at Popham Lane,* from *Tour in a Post Chaise,* pen and watercolor, 5 x 8 ins.
Figure 56. Thomas Rowlandson, *Mme. Catalani,* pen and watercolor, 9 x 7$\frac{1}{4}$ ins.
Figure 57. Thomas Rowlandson, *Concerto Spirituale,* pen and watercolor, 7$\frac{3}{4}$ x 6$\frac{1}{2}$ ins.
Figure 58. Thomas Rowlandson, *A French Frigate Towing an English Man-O-War into Port,* pen and watercolor, 10$\frac{1}{2}$ x 8$\frac{1}{4}$ ins.
Figure 59. William Blake, *Satan, Sin, and Death* (1808), pen and watercolor, 19$\frac{1}{2}$ x 15-13/16 ins.
Figure 60. William Blake, *Satan, Sin, and Death* (1807), pen and watercolor, 9$\frac{3}{4}$ x 8-3/16 ins.
Figure 61. William Hogarth, *Satan, Sin, and Death,* canvas, 24$\frac{3}{8}$ x 29$\frac{3}{8}$ ins. (The Tate Gallery, London).
Figure 62. Henry Fuseli, *Satan, Sin, and Death,* canvas, 26$\frac{1}{2}$ x 23 ins. (Los Angeles County Museum of Art).
Figure 63. James Barry, *Satan, Sin, and Death,* engraving.
Figure 64. James Barry, *Mercury Inventing the Lyre,* canvas, 27$\frac{1}{2}$ x 29$\frac{1}{2}$ ins. (Lord Egremont).
Figure 65. James Barry, *St. Sebastian,* pen and wash, 10$\frac{3}{4}$ x 6$\frac{3}{4}$ ins. (The National Gallery of Ireland).
Figure 66. William Blake, *Creation of Eve,* pen and watercolor, 10 x 8-3/16 ins.
Figure 67. John Flaxman, *And God Made the Firmament,* pen and wash, 4$\frac{1}{8}$ x 5$\frac{5}{8}$ ins.
Figure 68. William Blake, *David Delivered Out of Many Waters,* pen and watercolor, 16$\frac{3}{8}$ x 13$\frac{5}{8}$ ins. (The Tate Gallery, London).
Figure 69. Richard Wilson, *River Scene with Bathers,* canvas, 35$\frac{1}{8}$ x 56$\frac{1}{8}$ ins.
Figure 70. Richard Wilson, *Monte Cavo,* black and white chalk, 11$\frac{1}{2}$ x 16$\frac{3}{8}$ ins.
Figure 71. Richard Wilson, *Temple of Minerva Medica,* black and white chalk, 11$\frac{1}{4}$ x 16$\frac{1}{2}$ ins. (Mr. and Mrs. Paul Mellon).
Figure 72. Richard Wilson, *Landscape with Bathers,* canvas, 23 x 29$\frac{1}{2}$ ins. (The Tate Gallery, London).
Figure 73. Richard Wilson, *Landscape with Bathers,* canvas, 25 x 46 ins. (Leeds City Art Galleries).
Figure 74. Richard Wilson, *Dolbadarn Castle and Llyn Peris,* canvas, 37 x 50 ins. (The National Gallery of Victoria, Melbourne).
Figure 75. Richard Wilson, *Niobe,* canvas, 46 x 66 ins. (destroyed during World War II, photo courtesy The Tate Gallery, London).
Figure 76. Thomas Gainsborough, *The Cottage Door,* canvas, 58 x 47 ins.
Figure 77. Thomas Gainsborough, *The Cottage Door,* (detail).
Figure 78. Thomas Gainsborough, *The Cottage Door,* canvas, 47 x 58 ins. (Cincinnati Art Museum).

Figure 79. Thomas Gainsborough, *The Woodcutter's Return*, canvas, 58½ x 47½ ins. (Lady Oakes).

Figure 80. Thomas Gainsborough, *The Cottage Door*, canvas, 38¾ x 48¾ ins. (Mrs. Scudamore).

Figure 81. Thomas Gainsborough, *Cottage Door with Peasant Smoking*, canvas, 77 x 62 ins. (Kennedy Collection, University of California at Los Angeles).

Figure 82. George Morland, *The Farmyard*, canvas, 39½ x 55 ins.

Figure 83. Ben Marshall, *Sam with Sam Chifney, Jr., Up*, canvas, 40 x 50 ins.

Figure 84. John Constable, *View on the Stour near Dedham*, canvas, 51 x 74 ins.

Figures 85, 86, 87. John Constable, *Three Pages from the 1814 Sketchbook*, pencil, 3⅛ x 4¼ ins. (The Victoria and Albert Museum, London).

Figure 88. John Constable, *Barges on the Stour*, oil on paper, 10¼ x 12¼ ins. (The Victoria and Albert Museum, London).

Figure 89. John Constable, *View on the Stour*, canvas, 51 x 75¼ ins. (The Royal Holloway College).

Figure 90. John Constable, *Man Poling a Barge*, pencil, 3½ x 4¾ ins. (The Victoria and Albert Museum, London).

Figure 91. John Constable, *View on the Stour near Dedham*, (detail).

Figure 92. John Constable, *Elm Trees in Old Hall Park, East Bergholt*, pencil and wash, 23¼ x 19½ ins. (The Victoria and Albert Museum, London).

Figure 93. John Constable, *View on the Stour near Dedham*, (detail).

Figure 94. John Constable, *Cloud Study*, canvas, 12 x 18 ins. (The National Gallery of Victoria, Melbourne).

Figure 95. J. M. W. Turner, *Grand Canal, Venice*, canvas, 58¼ x 43½ ins.

Figures 96 and 97. J. M. W. Turner, *Two adjoining pages from Turner's 1819 Milan to Venice Sketchbook*, pencil (The British Museum, London).

Figure 98. J. M. W. Turner, *Grand Canal, Venice*, watercolor, 11 x 15½ ins. (Kurt F. Pantzer, Indianapolis).

Figure 99. J. M. W. Turner, *Juliet and Her Nurse*, canvas, 36 x 48 ins. (Mrs. Flora Whitney Miller, New York).

Figure 100. J. M. W. Turner, *Grand Canal, Venice*, (detail).

Figure 101. J. M. W. Turner, *Apollo and Daphne*, panel, 42½ x 77½ ins. (The Tate Gallery, London).

Figure 102. J. M. W. Turner, *The Parting of Hero and Leander*, canvas, 57½ x 93 ins. (The National Gallery, London).

Figure 103. J. M. W. Turner, *Snowstorm, Avalanche and Inundation*, canvas, 36 x 48¼ ins. (The Art Institute of Chicago).

Figure 104. J. M. W. Turner, *Calais Pier*, canvas, 67¾ x 94½ ins. (The National Gallery, London).

Figure 105. J. M. W. Turner, *Festival of the Vintage, Macon*, canvas, 57 x 92 ins. (Graves Art Gallery, Sheffield).

Figure 106. J. M. W. Turner, *Mouth of the Grand Canal*, watercolor, 8¼ x 12¼ ins. (Mr. and Mrs. Paul Mellon).

TEN BRITISH PICTURES

Chapter I

The Revolution
in Eighteenth Century Art

ART HISTORIANS have long recognized that a major and fundamental change in European art takes place in the middle of the eighteenth century, and that this change is particularly pronounced in England. There is, however, less agreement about the nature of this development and the direction in which it is moving. From a purely visual point of view the most obvious feature of late eighteenth-century art is bewildering variety. The type of coherence that is normally found in earlier phases of European art simply is not present. This variety is apparent in many ways, but is probably most evident in what art historians call the "style" of the works produced at that time.

Style, as the word is used in the study of art, is a phenomenon with which everyone is familiar in one form or another. Skirts and waistlines in women's dresses go up and down over a period of years; men's trousers are cut loose or tight; fins come and go on automobiles. In noticing such differences in the appearance of objects around us we are responding, in an elementary way, to changes in style. The study of style in the art historical sense is really no more than a subtle and elaborate application of these same principles of observation to art. The underlying assumption is that works produced at the same time in the same place will have a strong family resemblance, particularly apparent in the forms artists construct and in the way they manipulate the materials with which they work.

Art historians have sufficient confidence in the validity of this assumption that they do not hesitate to use stylistic evidence as a means of assigning the date, locality, and even the name of the artist to a work of art. Thus, to an eye trained in stylistic analysis, matters such as composition, modeling of figures, and use of suggested depth, may indicate that a painting comes from the seventeenth century, was produced in Holland, and is the work of Rembrandt. The same techniques, further refined, may enable a student to decide the particular phase of an artist's career to which a work belongs. For instance, Rembrandt's paintings of the 1630's are perceptibly different from those of the 1640's in the way

Fig. 1. François Boucher, *The Luncheo* from *The Noble Pastoral*, designed in 1 woven at the Beauvais tapestry works, 10 ft. 10 ins. x 11 ft.

Fig. 2. J. Schmitz, *Chest*, French, mid-eighteenth century.

he groups his figures, places them in space, and uses light and shadow. He was so consistent in these matters that it is normal procedure to assign a date to one of his paintings as a result of the study of these stylistic factors. Coherence of this type at any given time and place is a regular feature of European art through the mid-eighteenth century. The story of art from the time of ancient Greece down to about 1750 is to a great extent a description of the various style phases that follow one another through the centuries. The art of the first half of the eighteenth century, called the rococo, is the last of these widely-based international style epochs.

The rococo delights in compound, swinging curves that ripple restlessly over lightly colored surfaces. "Surface" is a key word, for the rococo is essentially an art of two dimensions in contrast to the spatial complexities which fascinated the preceding period, called the baroque. In subject matter rococo art is light-hearted and witty, amusing and sensuous, avoiding high seriousness and drama. France is usually regarded as the native habitat of the rococo, where the paintings and tapestries of men like Boucher and the furniture of the Louis XV period are an epitome of the style (*Figs. 1 and 2*). But works of essentially the same character were being produced simultaneously in Italy, Germany and England. A Venetian decorated chest, a Bavarian mid eighteenth-century church interior, a painting by Hogarth, all exhibit the same fascination with restless curvilinear design animating the surfaces, "leading the eye a wanton kind of chase."

In the second half of the eighteenth century this type of stylistic coherence breaks down all over Europe. This is not to say there are no forms and attitudes characteristic of the late eighteenth century; certainly there are. Yet it is impossible to find common stylistic or formal properties that unite all this material and establish it as a style epoch. Some features of the rococo remain, but other styles are developed at the same time. Many of these are borrowed from different periods and cultures — the classical and medieval past, the civilizations of China or India — a few are newly created. All coexist in the art at the end of the eighteenth and the beginning of the nineteenth centuries.

Look, for instance, at two portrait drawings, one by the Anglo-Swiss Henry Fuseli, and the other by George Romney's short-lived brother, Peter (*Figs. 3 and 4*). They are roughly contemporary, both executed within a few years of 1775. From the point of view of style, the Fuseli drawing is distinctly "linear," the Romney "painterly." That is, Fuseli has conceived the form primarily in terms of contour and has provided a sense of three-dimensionality by gradual shading within these outlines. Romney, on the other hand, builds the head entirely in terms of broad areas of tone and light and shadow, the characteristically baroque or "painterly" method of constructing form. Stylistically the two drawings are sharply different.

Examples of comparable diversity can be readily found amongst the works of other British draftsmen at the time: the highly "linear" constructions of Flaxman, Blake, and Rowlandson, against the much more "painterly" conceptions of Gainsborough, Morland, and Gillray. It is contrary to our assumptions about style as a historical phenomenon that such different works of art should be executed at the same time and in the same place.

Frequently these shifts in style carry with them equally striking contrasts in

Fig. 3. Henry Fuseli, *Johann Jakob Bodmer*, pencil, 17⅞ x 12½ ins.

Fig. 4. Peter Romney, *Sophia Brierley*, brown and blue wash, 10¾ x 7¾ ins.

Fig. 5. William Pars, *View of Rome*, waterc⦁
18⅞ x 28¾ ins.

Fig. 6. Thomas Gainsborough, *Boats on a Lake*,
grey wash heightened with white, 11⅞ x 15¹³/₁₆ ins.

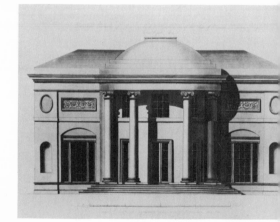

Fig. 8. James Wyatt, *Fonthill Abbey*, from John
Rutter, *Delineations of Fonthill and its abbey*
(London 1823).

Fig. 7. James Wyatt, *Design for Bowden*, f⦁
George Richardson, *The New Vitruvius
Britannicus* (London 1802).

the artists' aims and interests. William Pars' "View of Rome," for instance, is a painstakingly accurate depiction of buildings in that city seen from a viewpoint above the Tiber (*Fig. 5*). His intention is basically that of a reporter, to give us a clear, precise, factual record of the appearance of a special area. The buildings are drawn with the linear precision of an architectual draftsman, but enlivened by the artist's perception of light and color.

A landscape drawing by Gainsborough, on the other hand, represents not only another style but also a completely different conception of landscape (*Fig. 6*). The forms are broadly suggested in looping patterns of light and shadow. Equally important is the fact that the drawing is not a record of any particular place; rather it is a product of the artist's imagination. We know, from numerous contemporary references, that Gainsborough's normal practice was to arrange little scraps of moss, coal, and glass on his table, illuminate them with candles and use them as a stimulus to his imagination in the creation of landscape drawings. Of course, his vision was tempered by his rich store of recollections of actual trees, rocks and sunlight. But the fact is clear: the meaning of landscape for Gainsborough lay not in the accuracy with which it depicted a particular area, but in the gentle, lyrical mood he was able to create from these flowing, rhythmic forms as they emerged from his imagination. So the general intentions and interests of the artists in approaching landscape are here just as far apart as the styles they employ. For Pars, landscape drawing is something relatively empirical and direct; for Gainsborough, something conceptual, an idea residing in the mind of the artist rather than something actually observed.

A startling feature of this stylistic and ideological variety is that it frequently (at least in England) exists in the work of a single artist. Figures 7 and 8 show designs for two houses by James Wyatt. They are not precisely contemporary; Bowden dates from the 1780's, Fonthill from the 1790's. But there is no stylistic evolution involved from one to the other. Wyatt, as well as other contemporary architects such as John Nash, frequently worked simultaneously in such different modes.

There are so many differences between these two buildings that it would be tedious to try to enumerate them all. Stylistically they are at opposite poles. Consider such factors as the treatment of surface, the handling of the skyline, and the organization of the mass of the building. Even more fundamental than these differences in form are the differences in the ways the architect expected the spectator to respond to the structures. Bowden appeals basically to our sense of pattern and design. Proportion and balance, the careful creation of each element with an eye to its position in a well-ordered, harmonious whole — these are factors that here are uppermost in Wyatt's mind.

Fonthill Abbey operates in a different way. To be sure, we can also enjoy Fonthill as an abstract composition, responding to the dramatic silhouette and the massing of the component parts around the central tower. But if we stop there we miss a great deal of the interest and attraction Wyatt hoped the building would have. It is, of course, intended to look like and remind us of a medieval structure. And it is supposed to arouse by association thoughts concerning the glamour and excitement with which Wyatt and his contemporaries viewed the medieval past.

Appeal through visual associations is something the late eighteenth century knew a good deal about. All art, of course, appeals more or less by association and always has. We associate shapes and colors on canvas with human figures or trees. Even modern "abstract" paintings appeal to some extent through our associations with particular colors and shapes. But artists such as Wyatt are exploiting association in a slightly different way, or at least in a more sophisticated way. They appeal to our recollections of other art forms, often from remote periods and places, arousing thoughts of distant times and exotic objects.

This exploitation of the art of the past takes on considerable emphasis in the late eighteenth century. Artists have always looked to earlier art for help and guidance; they have mined it as a source for all sorts of ideas, and basically as a means of learning their trade by studying what their predecessors had done. Wyatt and his contemporaries understood and endorsed the use of earlier art in this way, particularly that of classical Greece and Rome and the Italian High Renaissance. But the period was also aware of other uses to which we can put the art of the past. Sir Joshua Reynolds states the issue very clearly when, in one of his Discourses to the students at the Royal Academy, he discusses the curious vogue then current for having portraits painted with the sitter wearing a Van Dyck dress — mimicking the costumes and poses of portraits a century or more earlier. "By this means," says Reynolds, "it must be acknowledged that very ordinary pictures acquired something of the air and effect of the works of Vandyck, and appeared therefore at first sight to be better pictures than they really were; they appeared so, however, to those only who had the means of making this association; and when made, it was irresistible."[1] Or, in another place, speaking more specifically of architecture, Reynolds states: "as we have naturally a veneration for antiquity, whatever building brings to our remembrance ancient customs and manners, such as the Castles of the Barons of ancient Chivalry, is sure to give this delight."[2] Clearly the late eighteenth-century artist understood and was prepared to exploit the power of images, forms and styles derived from other times and places to strike the spectator's imagination through association. And the willingness of the artists to play on these associations certainly contributes to the stylistic variety present in the art of that period.

One could go on at length summoning up examples such as those already mentioned to bolster the contention that, at least as far as England is concerned, there is no general stylistic coherence to be found in the art of the late eighteenth century. From this point of view, variety commands the field, and it is not merely superficial, but radical and thorough-going. Furthermore, the fact that this sort of contrast frequently is found within the work of a single artist, implies that it was planned and deliberate. We might even say that variety of the type described is one of the positive and fundamental characteristics of late eighteenth and early nineteenth-century art. It is a situation that causes the art historian concerned with style to pause. Rarely does one find such vacillation prior to the late eighteenth century and certainly at no earlier time would the type of variety within the work of one artist that we encounter in the building of Wyatt be widespread and accepted as a matter of course.

It must be clearly admitted that in spite of this variety it is still readily possible to identify a late eighteenth-century work of art, and also to identify the works of individual artists within that period. The bases on which we do so, however, are not stylistic in the generally used art-historical sense of the term. Certain motifs, subjects, and attitudes will be recognized as characteristic of the time. There are also "styles" in a more formal sense (such as neo-classic linearism and painterly picturesque) that, although totally dissimilar, occur primarily in the decades around 1800. Furthermore, individual artists have technical quirks that, like any form of handwriting, are highly personal and serve to identify the hand involved. All or any of these factors will reveal the origin of an object produced during the period under consideration. But they do not add up to a coherent style for the period that can be defined in terms of form — as we can, for instance, describe the styles of the high renaissance, the baroque, or the rococo. One is forced to the conclusion that at no earlier time in the history of art is there such radical variety in the forms produced by artists working at the same time under the same conditions.

Naturally this fascination with change isn't always as extreme as in the works of Wyatt, but it permeates a major part of the art and is a dominant concern of many artists. As early as the 1760's it appears to be a significant factor in the interiors designed by Robert Adam for Syon House. These do not exhibit the exaggerated contrasts of styles from different times and places that appear a little later in the works of Wyatt and Nash, but the conscious manipulations of color, surface and spatial treatment in the rooms can be accounted for only by a desire for differences in effect. The white and gray of the Entrance Hall (*Fig. 9*) is in dramatic contrast with the opulent display of color and rich materials in the adjoining Ante-room (*Fig. 10*). And the spatial effect of this room is deliberately complicated by the use of free-standing columns supporting gilded figures, and a full entablature, open in space, along one wall. The Dining Room, Drawing Room (*Fig. 11*) and Long Gallery (*Fig. 12*) each has richness of a different kind. The total effect of variety is accentuated by the fact that the visitor is expected to see the rooms in sequence, passing directly from one to the other.

These vacillations and adjustments for expressive effect are less immediately apparent in the work of individual painters than in architecture, but one need not look long or hard to find them. As early as the 1750's Richard Wilson moves freely from the landscape formulas of Claude to those of Salvator Rosa in accordance with the mood he wishes to create (*Figs. 69 and 75*). From the 1750's

Fig. 9. Robert Adam, *Entrance Hall at Syon House* (photo courtesy *Country Life*).

Fig. 10. Robert Adam, *Ante-room at Syon House* (photo courtesy *Country Life*).

Fig. 11. Robert Adam, *Drawing Room at Syon House* (photo courtesy *Country Life*).

Fig. 12. Robert Adam, *Long Gallery at Syon House* (photo courtesy *Country Life*).

on, Reynolds paints with various approaches to portraiture, some empirical and direct, some heavily dependent on the work of other artists (*Figs. 40 and 33*). J. M. W. Turner, especially in the first half of his career, is a complete master of a whole repertory of landscape styles, mostly derived from seventeenth-century painters (*Figs. 104 and 105*).

There are, however, notable painters during the period who do not exhibit this type of vacillation. Gainsborough comes to mind at once as an artist whose style, although it certainly changes and develops, does so in a traditional way and remains fundamentally consistent at any given point in his career. And in the early nineteenth century Constable, although intensely interested in exploring the various moods of his native countryside, does so within a basically consistent vocabulary. But generally one must concede that stylistic vacillation is widespread at the time, and one cannot describe late eighteenth-century art in terms of a single coherent style. In this respect the period differs fundamentally from those that preceded it in the long succession of style epochs. And it is in these terms that one is entitled to speak of a revolution during the eighteenth century in the attitude of artists toward the means for expression that they had at their disposal.

This variety is one of the most impressive visual characteristics of British, and indeed European, art from the mid-eighteenth to the mid-nineteenth century, the romantic period, as it is frequently called. The reasons for this situation are elusive, but a basic factor is certainly the desire of artists to explore and control the widest possible range of expression. Any one stylistic vocabulary was inadequate to convey the different emotions these artists assumed as their province. This aspiration toward universality of expression led the artists to examine in a more conscious and deliberate way than ever before the means at their disposal for creating contrasts in mood. A developing historical sense, along with an interest in the remote and exotic, led in particular to an awareness of period and regional styles as things that might be adopted at will. But this is only part of a general awareness of style or form as something that might be manipulated and adjusted depending on the expressive effect desired. This conscious awareness of styles (in the plural) and of form in general as things that can be changed is one of the most significant visual developments of the romantic period, at least in England.

Historically it is difficult to put precise chronological limits to this phenomenon. If the situation is regarded as having been created by the romantic longing for the full gamut of emotional expression, and if romanticism is considered as a state of mind rather than a historical period, then it might be expected that this attitude toward style and form would arise whenever the romantic temperament appears — and this seems to be the case.[3] But unquestionably the period when this outlook was most prevalent was from the mid-eighteenth to the mid-nineteenth century. As far as British art is concerned the phenomena we have been discussing became distinctly noticeable in the decades of the 1750's and 60's, with the development of the so-called revival styles in architecture, and the emergence as mature artists of men like Reynolds and Wilson, although the intellectual climate that nurtured this attitude goes back earlier. The outlook continued to evolve during the late eighteenth century to reach a climax in the first quarter of the nineteenth with the architecture of men such as Nash and the early paintings of Turner. By the 1840's a reaction of sorts set in. One of the first articulate counterblasts came from Augustus Welby Pugin, who, in 1843, began his fulminations against what he called "the carnival of architecture," and his advocacy of one style (Gothic) for essentially moral and ethical reasons.[4] Generally the intense stylistic variety characteristic of art in the years around 1800 simmered down in the second quarter of the nineteenth century. Even Turner became much more consistent stylistically after 1840. But once this conscious awareness of style has been mastered, it cannot be unlearnt, and it has remained with us ever since, one of the principal legacies, for better or for worse, of the romantic period to the visual arts in general.

It would be difficult to overestimate the significance of this shift in attitude that took place at the turn of the eighteenth to the nineteenth century. As far as the spectator is concerned it opened the way to a sympathetic interest in and enjoyment of art from many different periods and places, to the acceptance of various styles and artistic intentions as legitimate. All art was no longer measured by a single yardstick. It was realized that many artists were not trying to do comparable things, and that comparisons of their merits are not always possible or relevant. At the same time, the appeal through association carried with it hazards of its own: a sprinkling of classical columns, medieval battlements or Moorish minarets often disguised weakness of design in a building, just as an interesting story or an emotionally provocative situation might lead the spectator to overlook incompetent formal organization in a painting.

For the artists themselves the new developments had in the long run a liberating effect. They were free to explore a wider range of intention than had previously been acceptable in art, and among these possibilities were most of the ideas that subsequently were developed at one time or another in the later nineteenth century. The chapters that follow explore the unfolding of some of these ideas in English art through the study of a few paintings in the Huntington Collection.

[1]Sir Joshua Reynolds, *Discourses on Art*, ed. Robert R. Wark (San Marino, California, 1959), pp. 138-39.

[2]Ibid., pp. 241-42.

[3]For a discussion of a related phenomenon in ancient Roman art see Otto J. Brendel, "Prolegomena to a Book on Roman Art," *Memoirs of the American Academy in Rome*, XXI (1953), pp. 9-73.

[4]Augustus Welby Pugin, *An Apology for the Revival of Christian Architecture in England* (London, 1843), p. 2.

Fig. 13. William Hogarth, *Bishop Benjamin Hoadly*, canvas, 24 x 19 ins.

Chapter II
Hogarth's "Bishop Hoadly"

WILLIAM HOGARTH'S PORTRAIT of Bishop Benjamin Hoadly (*Fig. 13*) appears at first glance to be a straightforward, unassuming painting. Part of this effect comes from the small physical size (the picture is just two feet high). Also, the good-natured, roly-poly countenance of the bishop is reassuring and unpretentious in spite of the elaborate robes he is wearing and the rather grand accessories with which he is surrounded. It is a lively little painting, full of pleasure for the eye, especially in the rich pattern of compound curves created by the furniture and the drapery, in the application of the pigment, and in the subtle but decorative color organization. Simply from a visual standpoint the picture is entitled to our admiration. But when viewed within the context of Hogarth's artistic career and the development of British painting during the eighteenth century the portrait assumes additional significance.

Bishop Hoadly and Hogarth were good friends, and they shared a distinctly positive, rather pugnacious temperament. The bishop was one of the more spirited and controversial figures in the religious life of the period. Innumerable pamphlets streamed from his busy pen, mostly arguing some point of theology with one or another of his clerical colleagues. He advocated the Low Church, latitudinarian, Whig points of view, and consequently was in great favor at the court following the Hanoverian succession. He rose quickly in the ranks of the church hierarchy after the accession of George I. In December of 1715 he became Bishop of Bangor, an office he held for six years without ever visiting his see. In 1721 he was transferred to Hereford; in 1723 to Salisbury; and finally, in 1734, he became Bishop of Winchester. An honor that had long been associated with the see of Winchester was the post of Prelate of the Order of the Garter. It is in the robes of that office that Hogarth has painted his friend. The badge of the order is embroidered on the left shoulder of the bishop's cloak; "the George" hangs suspended from a ribbon around his neck; in the background is Windsor Castle, the seat of the Order of the Garter. At the time he became Bishop of Winchester, Hoadly was approaching sixty. The major portion of his career and most of his voluminous writings were behind him. He lived for another quarter century, but as a comparatively mellow old man.

Hogarth was about twenty years younger than the bishop, and indeed was closer in age to the bishop's children. Two of these, Benjamin (a doctor) and John (a poet and dramatist), must have been on fairly close terms with the painter. John composed verses that were engraved on the plates of Hogarth's "A Rake's Progress." Benjamin is said to have given help to the artist in the writing of his book, *The Analysis of Beauty*. Hogarth painted several portraits of young Benjamin, at least one of his brother John, and two of their father the bishop. Given the personal relationships between Hogarth and Bishop Hoadly, as well as the importance of the sitter, there is ample reason to believe that the artist would give special attention to the portrait of the prelate, and that it would not be regarded simply as a routine commission.

We are not sure precisely when the Huntington portrait of Bishop Hoadly was painted. Clearly it must have been after 1734 when he became Bishop of Winchester, and (for reasons to be considered later) it must have been before 1743. Probably the date is in the late 1730's. At any rate, the picture comes from a time when Hogarth was a well-established artist both in reputation and accomplishment. As a painting it is related to an art form called the "conversation piece," of which Hogarth made something of a specialty. These attractive little pictures, which were very popular in England during the second quarter of the eighteenth century, normally represented members of the same family or close friends shown together in an informal fashion, having tea, playing cards, or simply talking to one another. The figures (like Bishop Hoadly) were usually portrayed at full length, but very much under life size. There is, unfortunately, no example of a Hogarth conversation piece in the Huntington collection, but Francis Hayman's "Gascoigne Family" (*Fig. 14*) and Arthur Devis' group of the Lyttleton family (*Fig. 15*) are both excellent examples of what is meant by the term. The portrait of Bishop Hoadly together with the companion portrait of his wife (*Fig. 16*) form a unit that in the scale of the figures resembles a conversation piece in general effect.

The conversation piece had its immediate origins in early eighteenth-century France, although group portraits of a more general type were very popular in seventeenth-century Holland. The idea was brought to England about 1720 by artists of French training and extraction. It was a type of picture that had particular appeal for the English and was developed by them to a position of importance far beyond anything that it ever attained on the other side of the Channel. Hogarth himself was, with little doubt, the most distinguished exponent of this type of painting in England.

Many reasons — social, economic, and artistic — have been advanced for the popularity of the conversation piece. It is an art form associated largely with the middle class, a part of society that came much to the fore in early eighteenth-century England, and which doubtless found this informal, domestic style of portraiture congenial. The idea of obtaining a group of portraits on one canvas

Fig. 14. Francis Hayman, *The Gascoigne Family*, canvas, 40 x 50 ins.

Fig. 15. Arthur Devis, *Lord Lyttleton,
his brother and sister-in-law*, canvas,
49½ x 39½ ins.

Fig. 16. William Hogarth,
Mrs. Hoadly, canvas, 24 x 19 ins.

rather than paying for a whole series of single figures may also have appealed to the thrifty instincts of these self-made businessmen. But much more important is the fact that the conversation piece is an art form entirely typical of the style epoch that produced it — the rococo. Certainly the conversation piece does not exhibit the concern with playful and often mildly erotic themes that are an important component of continental rococo art; but the painter's arrangement of the figures, his handling of color, and light and shadow, as well as his generally decorative intention, are all in accord with that style. The rococo painter was interested in creating a graceful, rippling effect in his works. He built color areas in relatively high intensities that meet each other abruptly with little shading or transition. Furthermore he distributed these colors over the whole space of the canvas. The result is a lively, sparkling, animated surface. But the elimination of modeling and gradual tonal transitions means that the eye "reads" a rococo painting primarily as a surface rather than representations of solids in suggested depth. It is a style that lends itself admirably to the depiction of light-hearted, fluttering subjects, but is not an adequate vehicle through which to convey powerful emotions.

The Huntington painting of Bishop Hoadly reflects in certain respects the rococo conversation piece tradition; but it also gives evidence of Hogarth's interest (at this mid-point in his career) in exploring other forms of portraiture. It is in the scale, the pictorial organization, and (most of all) in the way the paint is applied to the canvas that the affiliations with the rococo are most apparent. But the setting and general accoutrements with which the bishop is surrounded suggest a desire for something more grand and monumental than normally appears in the conversation piece. The introduction of the column and great sweep of drapery both add a rhetorical note, as does the presence of Windsor Castle in the background, alluding to the Order of the Garter.

The significance of these departures from the rococo conversation piece tradition in Hogarth's portrait of Hoadly is apparent when one turns to the artist's great portrait of Captain Coram (*Fig. 17*), painted in 1740, probably very shortly after the Huntington "Bishop Hoadly." The portrait of Captain Coram has long been recognized as one of the key paintings in Hogarth's career and a major document in the history of English portraiture. Thomas Coram was a retired sea captain who decided to devote his fortune and energies to charitable purposes, notably the establishment of an institution to care for orphans, the Foundling Hospital. It was an enterprise that also had the support of Coram's friend Hogarth, who encouraged leading London artists to contribute paintings to adorn the walls of the public rooms of the building. Hogarth's own initial contribution was a portrait of the founder.

The relations between Hogarth's portraits of Bishop Hoadly and Captain Coram are fascinating. There is, of course, a very important difference in size. The Captain Coram is life scale; the picture is nearly eight feet high, as com-

Fig. 17. William Hogarth, *Captain Coram*, canvas, 94 x 58 ins. (Thomas Coram Foundation for Children, London).

pared with the twenty-four inches of "Bishop Hoadly." The "Captain Coram" is indeed Hogarth's first and only attempt at a full-length, life-scale portrait. He otherwise used life scale only for portraits of the head-and-shoulder or three-quarter length type. But if the Hoadly and Coram portraits are radically different in physical size, the compositions have a great deal in common. There seems little doubt that Hogarth must have had his picture of Bishop Hoadly very much in mind when he began work on "Captain Coram," and that the small painting provides the genesis of the artistic ideas developed in the large one.

There are different ways in which one can approach and interpret the portrait of Captain Coram. It has frequently been seen as an heroic presentation of a middle-class sitter, an attempt to create an air of dignity and monumentality without disguising the essentially bourgeois character of the subject. One may also approach the portrait more from the standpoint of style, and see it as an attempt to break away from the rococo conventions of painting. There is nothing incompatible about these two ways of looking at the picture, and indeed they are simply different ways of saying the same thing. From all that we have observed about the rococo as a style, it clearly is not the ideal vehicle for expressions of monumentality and dignity, or for strong emotional content of any sort. There is much that is still essentially rococo about "Captain Coram" — the curvaceous contours of the coat, the scattered light and shadow accents (especially the artfully placed clutter in the right foreground), and the lack of insistence on effects of depth or mass. But there is, in the appearance of elements such as the column and great sweep of drapery in the right background, evidence of a desire to modify rococo form in favor of greater stability and dignity. In these intentions the portrait of Bishop Hoadly anticipates that of Captain Coram. Insofar as "Captain Coram" is among the first of the great full-length exhibition portraits that became one of the chief glories of British painting in the generation following Hogarth, then the portrait of Bishop Hoadly may be regarded as a modest but prophetic indication of what is to come.

The extent to which the portrait of Captain Coram (or that of Bishop Hoadly) may be regarded as a complete artistic success is a matter of opinion. The good-natured captain and the pugnacious bishop don't look completely at ease among the grand-manner accessories with which they are surrounded. There is a degree of tension between the figure and the setting, just as there is an element of conflict between the restless, fluttering rococo form and the desire for something more dignified and stable. This tension between Hogarth's artistic aims and the rococo style is found in much of his work and is a factor of great interest to the historian of art. It is apparent even in the series of narrative paintings for which Hogarth is most famous, such as "The Harlot's Progress," "The Rake's Progress," and "Marriage à la Mode." Hogarth began painting these narrative series in the early 1730's, and continued to produce them from time to time through the rest of his career. In physical size and general appearance they are not unlike the conversation piece portraits. And as many of the narrative pictures also include portraits, the line of division between them and the conversation pieces is often difficult to draw. Stylistically, both are rococo paintings; some of the narrative pictures (particularly the early scenes of "Marriage à la Mode") deserve to be considered the major masterpieces of rococo art produced in England. Yet in general intention these series transcend the limitations of the rococo. Hogarth tells us on more than one occasion that his aim in these series is moral and didactic, to point out (and hopefully correct) various social evils. This is a lofty and serious purpose. But I think it is doubtful (in spite of the brilliance of individual paintings) whether Hogarth successfully attains this ethical aim. The root of the trouble may once again be a lack of harmony between the artist's objectives and the rococo style with which he is working.

Consider the series "Marriage à la Mode," painted in the early 1740's within three or four years of "Bishop Hoadly" and "Captain Coram" (*Figs. 18-23*). The six paintings constitute Hogarth's finest accomplishment in story telling and represent his work at the very peak of his powers. The pictures relate the tale of a marriage between the daughter of a wealthy merchant and the son of a spendthrift nobleman. The story unfolds in six scenes. The first is the signing of the marriage contract, a frank exchange of money for social position, a transaction engineered entirely by the fathers of the two young people. Scene two shows the young couple shortly after marriage, already pursuing independent dissipations. There follow two pictures exploring in more detail the downward path of first the husband and then his wife. The climax of the series comes in scene five when the husband, suspecting his wife's infidelity, follows her and her paramour to a bagnio and is there killed in a duel. In the final episode the wife takes poison on learning that her lover has died on the gallows.

The first four scenes are concerned more with humor than pathos. An ominous note creeps in with three and four, although it is all but smothered under the welter of anecdotal detail and visual titillation. These are rococo paintings *par excellence;* witty, and slightly naughty pictures in which the thematic material is in complete harmony with the restless, sparkling surface of the paint. But scenes five and six present (or one suspects were intended to present) a different situation. Five in particular is the dramatic and emotional climax of the story, the point at which Hogarth should drive home the moral. The scene does not really carry this impact, although I think it is clear, simply from a visual standpoint, that Hogarth is making some adjustments in that direction. The episode is set in a semi-dark room with the result that there is little of the sparkling color that gives the other paintings such a gay effect. Hogarth also concentrates the light on the two central figures for additional attention. He underlines the broken, falling character of the young man's body with the sword, in mid-air, emphasizing the unnatural angle of the legs.

There is every reason to believe that Hogarth was consciously aware of these

Fig. 18. William Hogarth, *Marriage à la Mode*,
Scene I, canvas, 27 x 35 ins.
(The National Gallery, London).

Fig. 19. William Hogarth, *Marriage à la Mode*,
Scene II, canvas, 27 x 35 ins.
(The National Gallery, London).

Fig. 20. William Hogarth, *Marriage à la Mode*,
Scene III, canvas, 27 x 35 ins.
(The National Gallery, London).

Fig. 21. William Hogarth, *Marriage à la Mode*,
Scene IV, canvas, 27 x 35 ins.
(The National Gallery, London).

Fig. 22. William Hogarth, *Marriage à la Mode*,
Scene V, canvas, 27 x 35 ins.
(The National Gallery, London).

Fig. 23. William Hogarth, *Marriage à la Mode*,
Scene VI, canvas, 27 x 35 ins.
(The National Gallery, London).

visual adjustments, and made them for dramatic effect. In his book *The Analysis of Beauty* Hogarth reveals himself as an artist who thinks very much of the expressive potentialities of abstract organization in a picture in addition to the things and situations represented. He speaks in particular about lines and the extent to which the essential expression of a figure can be conveyed by a linear abstraction of the basic axes and contours. Thus figures of ideal beauty may be schematically represented by a gently modulated S curve. And characters differing from the ideal may be represented almost in abstract form by lines that are "in attitudes of authority more extended and spreading than ordinary, but reduced somewhat below the medium of grace in those of negligence or ease; and as much exaggerated in insolent and proud carriage or in distortions of pain as lessened and contracted into parallel lines to express meanness, awkwardness, and submission."[1] There are also indications in the *Analysis* that Hogarth is aware of the expressive potentialities of light and shadow as well as general composition in a painting.[2]

Hogarth's thinking concerning means of expression in a painting and the importance of abstract organization are essentially valid. There is little doubt that he was intellectually aware of the best way to proceed in order to obtain the more emotionally concentrated effect one suspects he wanted in a picture such as Scene V of "Marriage à la Mode." There are several reasons why the scene does not carry the punch it should. The primary difficulties are that the gestures and actions of the figures are overly theatric and artificial, and there are too many extraneous trivia. The eye is still distracted from the principal group by all sorts of anecdotal details that compete for our attention. Or, to make substantially the same observation in different terms, the painting still retains much of the rococo scattered, overall surface animation, and this dissipates the visual impact. Once again, as with the portraits of Bishop Hoadly and Captain Coram, there is a degree of tension between the rococo style that dominates Hogarth's work and the desire of the artist for a deeper and richer emotional content. But in seeking to strengthen and vary the emotional character of his paintings Hogarth points clearly towards attitudes developed by artists in the latter part of the eighteenth century.

For those who enjoy minor puzzles and conundrums there are a couple of additional problems connected with the portrait of Bishop Hoadly that invite attention. Hogarth painted two portraits of the bishop. The second, which is in London's Tate Gallery, shows Hoadly at three-quarter length, but life scale (*Fig. 24*). There are many differences between the two pictures in addition to the physical size, but there is also a striking and important connection. The portions of the figure common to both paintings are, with a few details excepted, mirror images of one another. This relationship, which is particularly apparent in the folds of the bishop's robes, is much too close to be dismissed as accidental. The detection of this sort of connection between two works of art always sets

Fig. 24. William Hogarth, *Bishop Benjamin Hoadly*, canvas, 49½ x 39½ ins.
(The Tate Gallery, London).

The Right Reverend Father in GOD, Dr. BENJAMIN HOADLY, LORD BISHOP OF WINCHESTER Prelate of the Most Noble Order of the Garter. Æt. 67. A.D. 1743.

Fig. 25. B. Baron, after Hogarth, *Bishop Benjamin Hoadly*, engraving.

the connoisseur's nose quivering. Usually one expects that some sort of a print acts as the intermediary between the two. An engraved plate, like nearly all printing mechanisms, yields an impression that is the reverse of the original design. Once such a print has been made it can serve as the source for another painting, which will then bear a mirror relationship to the first. An engraving was issued in 1743 by the print maker Baron that is very close to the Tate painting (*Fig. 25*). Clearly these three objects, the Huntington portrait, the Tate portrait, and the Baron engraving, must be connected in a chronological sequence. The problem is to determine the order in which they come. If Baron had engraved his plate from the Tate picture one would normally expect the resulting print to be backwards, a mirror image. Of course, like many print-makers at that time, he could have avoided this reversal by making use of a mirror or some related device in cutting his plate, so that the impression would read in the same direction as the original. There are, however, one or two details in the print that suggest Baron did not work this way, and that the picture he used as his source faced in the same direction as the Huntington portrait. Most signifi-cant is the fact that the motto of the Order of the Garter, 'Honi soit qui mal y pense,' on the badge on the bishop's shoulder, reads backwards on the print. It is also puzzling that the bishop is apparently giving a blessing with his left hand in both the print and the Tate painting. The probability seems very strong that the source from which Baron engraved his print must have been a picture in which the bishop faced in the same direction as in the Huntington portrait. There are, however, a sufficient number of discrepancies between the Hunting-ton picture and the print — particularly in the background and the disposition of the hands — that it is unlikely Baron worked directly from that painting. Probably he, or Hogarth, made an intermediate drawing that acted as the engraver's immediate source. But this hypothetical solution leaves the Tate painting curiously dangling, and implies that Hogarth painted the portrait working from a print based on one of his own paintings! In view of the fact that Hogarth was a friend of the bishop and could presumably have asked him to sit for another portrait at any time, this explanation concerning how the Tate painting came into being is clearly not very satisfactory. No really acceptable solution to this puzzle seems to be forthcoming. The Baron print does, however, supply a date before which the Huntington portrait must have been completed, 1743. Whatever explanation is ultimately found for the connection between the two paintings, the Huntington version must precede the print, and may well have done so by several years. If the suggested relation between the Hunt-ington "Bishop Hoadly" and "Captain Coram" is correct, then the former picture probably comes from the late 1730's, just before Hogarth started work on his heroic portrait of the captain.

Yet a further problem connected with the Huntington picture is the com-panion portrait of Mrs. Hoadly (*Fig. 16*). The bishop was married twice. His first wife, Sarah Curtis, died in 1743. She was a portrait painter in her own right, a pupil of Mary Beale. Her portrait of her husband, in the National Portrait Gallery, is supposed to have been touched up by Hogarth. The bishop's second marriage was with Mary, daughter of John Newey, dean of Chichester, and this took place in 1745. If the Huntington portrait of the bishop was painted just before 1740, then it is logical to assume that the lady is the first wife, Sarah. But there are a few complications. The portrait of the lady is not so impressive a painting as that of the bishop. Nor is the difference simply one of quality. The physical build-up of the painting, including the priming and pigment layers, is different. It is difficult to understand why an artist painting two portraits at the same time that were clearly intended as pendants should adopt such different painting procedures. One possible explanation is that the portraits were not in fact executed at the same time; that the lady was painted sometime later as a companion to the existing picture. This thought opens the possibility that the lady might be the bishop's second wife, Mary.

There are thus many interesting facets to the Huntington portrait of Bishop Hoadly in addition to its immediate attraction as a very accomplished little painting. For those who are amused by detective work the problems of its relations with the Tate portrait and the pendant portrait of Mrs. Hoadly remain unsolved. But much more important than these riddles is the fact that the painting exemplifies one of the most significant artistic factors in Hogarth's career, the tension that developed between the rococo style which was his essential mode of painting and his desire for wider and deeper emotional expression than was possible within that idiom, a desire that points clearly in the direction taken by later eighteenth-century art.

[1]William Hogarth, *The Analysis of Beauty*, ed. Joseph Burke (Oxford, 1955), pp. 145-46.

[2]For a more expanded discussion of this problem see Robert R. Wark, "Hogarth's Narrative Method in Practice and Theory," *England in the Restoration and Early Eighteenth Century*, (to be published by the University of California Press, 1971).

Fig. 26. Thomas Gainsborough, *The Blue Boy*, canvas, 70 x 48 ins.

Chapter III

Gainsborough's "The Blue Boy"

No OTHER PAINTING by a British artist enjoys the popularity of "The Blue Boy." And it deserves its fame, for the picture is one of the most remarkable productions of a painter who is in many respects the best that England has produced. Yet this great popularity is a doubtful asset. Few paintings have been more frequently reproduced than "The Blue Boy"; it has appeared in every conceivable form: on playing cards, candy-box covers, cocktail napkins, porcelain plates, highball glasses, and ash trays. The same familiar figure may emerge as a statuette, as a needlepoint picture, or dimly in the background of a clothier's advertisement telling the public to take a hint from Thomas Gainsborough and wear blue. The result of this activity is that for most people the painting is so entangled with irrelevant associations that it is almost impossible to have any direct reaction to it as a work of art. In a word, the image is hackneyed.

The original painting itself is certainly the most potent antidote to the dulling effect of innumerable copies. Anyone in the presence of the original is immediately struck by its power and assurance, so different from the cloying sentimentality that frequently hangs about the reproductions. The painting, like most fine works of art, appeals in different ways. Many visitors enjoy it simply for what it represents: a handsome young man in a handsome costume. Others find pleasure in Gainsborough's performance as a painter: the vigorous brushwork that builds the firmly modeled figure; the skillful way in which the cool blue of the costume is given vitality by being placed against the stormy sky. Still others (with a leaning toward the history of art) are impressed by the unusual qualities of the painting when seen in relation to other portraits by Gainsborough; for there can be little doubt that this was no routine portrait commission but a picture the artist painted with special enthusiasm. From whatever point of view we approach the painting it is certainly one of the most memorable of Gainsborough's achievements, well entitled to a place of honor in the select company of major British portraits. There is, however, no single explanation for why the painting attained such a preeminent place in popular esteem. The basis of this appeal is certainly the painting's intrinsic quality as a work of art. But supplementing this are factors such as the particular attraction of portraits of children for the nineteenth-century public, the slight air of mystery that surrounds the identity of the sitter, the extensive public exposure of the painting in exhibitions, and the excitement surrounding its purchase and export from England.

Stories and anecdotes envelop a work of art much as ivy does a building. They often add to the charm but at the same time may obscure and even damage what they are intended to enhance. A painting as famous as "The Blue Boy" naturally has a great many stories clinging about it. These involve almost every aspect of the picture: the identity of the young man represented; the place of the painting within Gainsborough's career; the special circumstances that governed the creation of the portrait; and the history of what has happened to it since the eighteenth century. Many of these stories are true, but others are only half-true or false. The latter, by building a sham environment around the work of art, get in the way of our proper understanding and enjoyment of it. The account that follows is an attempt to present the evidence and set the record straight, with the hope that the way may thus be cleared for a more sympathetic and enlighened approach to the painting itself.

In spite of the great reputation "The Blue Boy" has enjoyed during the last century and a half, the picture does not appear to have attracted much attention during Gainsborough's lifetime. There are no absolutely certain contemporary references that answer any of the basic questions about it. The evidence concerning the identity of the sitter dates from twenty years after Gainsborough's death, but nevertheless it is reasonably convincing. In 1808 a volume appeared by Edward Edwards entitled *Anecdotes of Painters*. "The Blue Boy" is mentioned in the book (p. 140), and a footnote is added stating: "This was the portrait of a Master Brutall, whose father was then a very considerable ironmonger, in Greek-street, Soho." Edwards was an associate of the Royal Academy. He was only eleven years younger than Gainsborough, with whom he was probably acquainted. Certainly he had opportunity to meet people who knew Gainsborough well. His comments, accordingly, have the authority of a contemporary source. Edwards died in December 1806, and his book was seen through the press by someone else, but there is no evidence that the editors tampered with the text.

Edwards has misspelled the name, but he is clearly referring to a certain Jonathan Buttall, who, like his father, was an ironmonger (or hardware merchant) in Greek Street in the Soho area of London. We do not know much about Buttall, aside from the fact that he was a personal friend of Gainsborough and (according to the artist's biographer William Whitley) one of the very select group that the painter requested should attend his funeral. The Buttalls owned property in Ipswich, where Gainsborough lived as a young man, and it is possible accordingly that the friendship was of long standing. Buttall ran into financial difficulties in the 1790's, and his possessions were sold at auction on Thursday, December 15, 1796. The sale was attended by the artist Joseph Farington, who noted in his diary: "Gainsboroughs picture of a Boy in a Blue Vandyke dress sold for 35 guineas." This is the earliest explicit reference to the painting so far located. But evidently Farington did not know that the sitter was Jonathan Buttall himself. Buttall died late in 1805 and was buried on December 6 at St. Anne Soho. According to the "Account of Burials" for the church he was 53 at the time of his death.

The question of when Gainsborough painted "The Blue Boy" is more elusive than the identity of the sitter. On general stylistic grounds it is clear that the painting must date from the middle phase of the artist's career, sometime after the mid-1760's but before the 1780's. Gainsborough's early, conversation piece style, represented in the Huntington collection by "A Lady with a Spaniel" (*Fig. 27*), has great charm but lacks the easy assurance and aristocratic elegance of "The Blue Boy." Likewise his late work, of which the Huntington Gallery's "Lady Petre" (*Fig. 28*) is a characteristic example, has a diaphanous and filmy quality arising from economic and fluid brushwork, all of which is very different from the comparatively thickly applied paint and solidly modeled form in "The Blue Boy." At the time Gainsborough executed the painting his art was balanced between the two extreme positions. At this stage of his career he was resident in Bath, the fashionable resort town in the west of England. The change from

Fig. 27. Thomas Gainsborough, *Lady with a Spaniel*, canvas, 30 x 25 ins.

Fig. 28. Thomas Gainsborough, *Lady Petre*, canvas, 88¾ x 57¼ ins.

his early to his late style was to a great extent dictated by the changing demands of his patrons. What pleased and suited the country gentry around Ipswich (where he worked as a young artist) would not satisfy the world of fashion at Bath and London. But the change was also prompted by Gainsborough's contact with the portraits of the seventeenth-century painter Sir Anthony Van Dyck (*Fig. 29*). Gainsborough had unbounded admiration for the work of Van Dyck, and the younger man found a congenial model in the formula for portraying the English aristocracy that had been perfected by his predecessor over a century earlier. It was during Gainsborough's residence in Bath that the influence of Van Dyck was paramount, primarily in the format he adopted for his portraits and in the sense of dignity and aristocratic grace he was able to suggest in his sitters. Nevertheless it is unusual, at any stage of his career, to find the painter modeling himself so deliberately on Van Dyck as he does in "The Blue Boy"; even the costume, as well as the format and the pose, are derived from the seventeenth-century master. It is also rare at any time for Gainsborough to apply his paint so densely.

So the internal stylistic evidence presented by Gainsborough's own work does not enable us to go very far in suggesting when he painted "The Blue Boy" — the picture is too unusual to be easily pigeonholed. It may be worth noting, however, that Gainsborough uses again what certainly appears to be the same Van Dyck costume in two other portraits that can be firmly dated. The similarities (especially in the cut of the sleeve and shoulder) are too close to be accidental. One of these, the Hon. Edward Bouverie (*Fig. 30*), is inscribed 1773 and was paid for in September 1774. The other, Paul Cobb Methuen, was paid for in 1776. One is inclined to assume, on examining the dress in the three portraits, that Gainsborough must have actually had a Van Dyck costume in his studio, available for sitters who (in accordance with a curious fashion of the day) wanted their portraits painted in "fancy dress." This suggestion does not help much in dating "The Blue Boy," although Gainsborough was at least using the costume in his portraits of the early 1770's. The theory that Gainsborough kept a Van Dyck costume in his studio is given considerable support by some of his portraits of ladies in fancy dress from the 1770's (notably the Hon. Mrs. Graham, the Hon. Frances Duncombe, and Lady Margaret Fordyce) which utilize what is unquestionably the same woman's costume and hat, although the colors change.

A more specific point in the matter of dating is that Gainsborough did undoubtedly exhibit a portrait of a man in Van Dyck dress at the Royal Academy in 1770. For this we have the evidence of an academician, Mary Moser, who when describing the exhibition in a letter to Henry Fuseli said, among other things, "Gainsborough [is] beyond himself in a portrait of a gentleman in a Vandyke habit." It is unfortunate that Mary was not a little more explicit. The catalog of the Royal Academy exhibition of 1770 indicates that Gainsborough

Fig. 29. Sir Anthony Van Dyck, *George and Francis Villiers*, canvas, 54 x 50¼ ins. (H. M. Queen Elizabeth II).

Fig. 30. Thomas Gainsborough, *Hon. Edward Bouverie*, canvas, 29½ x 24½ ins. (private collection, England).

showed four male portraits that year, two full-lengths and two at three-quarters. One of the latter has been identified as a portrait of David Garrick, the actor; one of the former (No. 85) is particularized in the catalog as a portrait of a young gentleman. If Mary's comment referred to No. 85, then the painting was very probably "The Blue Boy," as we have no record of any other full-length portrait of a boy in a Van Dyck costume that could have been painted by Gainsborough prior to 1770. But unfortunately Mary does not say whether or not it was a "young" man she saw, or whether the portrait was full-length.

There is, however, one third-hand, rather flimsy bit of evidence from a much later date supporting the suggestion that it was indeed "The Blue Boy" that so impressed Mary Moser at the exhibition of 1770. J. T. Smith, the highly entertaining biographer of the sculptor Joseph Nollekens, records in *A Book for a Rainy Day* that on the third of November 1832 he was visited by his friend, the artist John Taylor, then in his ninety-third year. The conversation turned to Gainsborough. Taylor remarked: " 'Oh! I remember him; he was an odd man at times. I recollect my master Hayman coming home after he had been to an exhibition, and saying what an extraordinary picture Gainsborough had painted of the Blue Boy; it is as fine as Van Dyke.' " Smith then inquired who the Blue Boy was. " 'Why, he was an ironmonger, but why so called I don't know. He lived at the corner of Greek and King Streets, Soho; an immensely rich man.' " So Taylor also thought the Blue Boy was Jonathan Buttall. More important, however, is his recollection of Hayman's comment. Francis Hayman died in 1776. As far as one can gather from the exhibition records, the only full-length of a boy by Gainsborough that he would have seen was No. 85 in the Royal Academy exhibition of 1770. Although third-hand, and remote in time, the statement strongly supports the suggestion that "The Blue Boy" was in the 1770 exhibition.

Yet another detail, inconclusive in itself but further bolstering the presence of the picture in the 1770 exhibition, is a sketch in the Victoria and Albert Museum (E39-1920). The drawing, by an unknown artist, is clearly based on "The Blue Boy." It is inscribed in the same chalk as the sketch itself: "From Mr. T. Gainsborough/May 70." A plausible suggestion is that the sketch and inscription are notations made by an artist when he saw "The Blue Boy" in the 1770 exhibition.

Of course, if we accept the identification of the boy as Jonathan Buttall, then his lifespan offers evidence concerning the date of the painting. If Buttall was 53 at his death late in 1805, then he was born in 1752 or the last days of 1751. It is notoriously difficult to determine the age of a sitter from his appearance in a portrait, but there surely will be general agreement that the Blue Boy is — at the oldest — in his teens. If the sitter is Jonathan Buttall, then a date for the painting after 1770 would seem most improbable.

Much more interesting and important than the antiquarian problems concerning the identification of the sitter and the date is the question of whether or not any special circumstances account for the unusual character of the painting within Gainsborough's output.

One particularly attractive and persistent story concerning the origin of the painting suggests that Gainsborough undertook the picture to prove that his great contemporary rival, Sir Joshua Reynolds, was wrong when he stated that a cool color, such as blue, should never be the dominant area in a painting. The story fits so well with the very positive character of the painting and with what we know of the personalities of the two artists that one wishes it might be true. But unfortunately the only recorded statement by Reynolds that could serve as a basis for the story is included in one of his discourses to the Royal Academy delivered in 1778, well after the time when "The Blue Boy" must have been painted. Furthermore, the anecdote is not mentioned by any of Gainsborough's early biographers, several of whom knew him personally and would surely not have neglected such a fascinating and revealing episode if it had any foundation in fact. The story appears to have emerged in print first in John Young's *A Catalogue of the Pictures at Grosvenor House* (1821): "This Picture was painted in consequence of a dispute between Gainsborough, Sir Joshua Reynolds, and several other Artists. The former having asserted that he thought the predominant colour in a Picture ought to be blue; the others were of the opinion that it was not possible to produce a fine picture on such a principle; and the Artist in consequence painted this Portrait as an illustration of his opinion. It was considered that he had proved his assertion; and his performance having excited great attention, and become a general theme of praise with the Artists of that day, tended much to enhance the reputation he had already acquired." The anecdote grew with appropriate elaboration as time went on.

There is, however, another story concerning the origin of the painting that comes from an early and ascertainable source. This account was printed in the *European Magazine* for August 1798, and the author has been identified by Whitley (in his *Artists and Their Friends*) as William Seward, a friend of Reynolds and Samuel Johnson, well acquainted with the cultural life of London during the late eighteenth century. The notice reads: "Mr. Gainsborough. One of the finest portraits that this great artist ever painted, and which might be put upon a par with any portrait that was ever executed, is that of a boy in a blue Vandyke dress, and which is now in the possession of a tradesman in Greek-street. Gainsborough had seen a sketch of a Boy by Titian for the first time; and, having found a model that pleased him, he set to work with all the enthusiasm of his genius. 'I am proud,' said he, 'of being of the same profession with Titian, and was resolved to attempt something like him.' The famous large picture of Vandyke at Wilton was in general the model to which Gainsborough pointed, and he had arrived at a great facility in imitating that master."

The passage is puzzling as it leaves the reader uncertain about whether Seward thought the real inspiration for the picture was the work of Titian or of Van Dyck. Actually there is very little that is specifically Titianesque about "The

Fig. 31. Thomas Gainsborough, *The Blue Boy*, (detail).

Blue Boy." The paint application, especially on the left sleeve, and the rich glow of the blue color do remind one of the great Venetian, but all the references are emphatically to Van Dyck in pose, format, and costume (*Fig. 29*). There is, however, something very attractive and persuasive in Seward's suggestion (as in the anecdote about the dispute with Reynolds) that the painting was executed in answer to some sort of artistic challenge rather than simply as a regular commission. And there is in fact some specific evidence, not available to these early commentators, that strongly confirms the suggestion that the painting was not undertaken as a normal portrait.

X-ray photographs have revealed at least the beginning of another portrait of an older man beneath that of the Blue Boy (*Figs. 31 and 32*). It is clear from

Fig. 32. Thomas Gainsborough, *The Blue Boy*, (x-ray detail).

the position of the head of the older man that Gainsborough had planned the canvas as a normal full-length, which he subsequently cut down when he painted "The Blue Boy." We know nothing about this earlier painting — who was represented, or why Gainsborough never completed the work. But these problems are (as far as our discussion is concerned) less significant than the fact that "The Blue Boy" is painted on a piece of canvas that Gainsborough had used before. It is unlikely that a portrait painter beginning a new commission, with the sitter presumably in the studio, would pick up a used piece of canvas. The circumstance of the used, cut-down canvas strongly suggests that the painting was undertaken primarily for the artist's own satisfaction.

It is most improbable that we will ever now find out definitely whether or

· 37 ·

not "The Blue Boy" was painted to meet a special challenge. But from the bits of evidence at hand a tentative deduction is at least possible: Gainsborough (in answer to the demands of his patrons for portraits in fancy dress) had a Van Dyck costume made to keep in his studio. The artist's young friend, Jonathan Buttall, modeled the costume. (He may have even continued to act as the studio "sit-in" for the other portraits, all somewhat later, using the same dress.) Gainsborough, struck by the model's appearance, picked up a discarded canvas and tried an essay in the style of Van Dyck. If this line of reasoning is correct, then it is clear we should regard "The Blue Boy" as distinctly apart from the artist's normal commissioned portraits. Rather it is a *jeu d'esprit*, Gainsborough's homage to his mentor, an artist whom he admired above all others. Thus the picture should be classed along with Gainsborough's landscapes and so-called "fancy pictures" as something painted for his own pleasure.

It is interesting in this connection that in one of the very earliest comments on "The Blue Boy" the painting's peculiar power is attributed to the direct influence of Van Dyck. In 1798, William Jackson, in an essay on Gainsborough included in *The Four Ages*, criticizes the artist's "thin washy colouring" and "hatching style of pencilling," but then goes on to say, with specific reference to "The Blue Boy," "when, from accident or choice, he painted in the manly substantial style of Vandyke, he was very little, if at all, his inferior." Jackson's remark is of special interest because he was a personal friend of Gainsborough. Yet it would be misleading to give the impression that "The Blue Boy" owes all its distinction to the earlier artist. The references to Van Dyck, though emphatic and unmistakable, in no way dim the strength of Gainsborough's own personality, which shines through with a warmth, energy, and directness that creates a very different total impression from the comparatively cool aristocratic detachment characteristic of Van Dyck's English work.

Normally Gainsborough did not participate in the wholesale borrowing from earlier works of art that was a frequent device used by Reynolds and other contemporaries as a means of enriching the emotional appeal of their paintings. But "The Blue Boy," which was clearly intended to derive part of its attraction from the reference to Van Dyck, indicates Gainsborough's awareness of the appeal through association that was exploited by many of his contemporaries.

A NOTE ON THE HISTORY OF THE PAINTING

Leaving aside the 1770 comment of Mary Moser which may or may not refer to "The Blue Boy," the earliest explicit mention of the painting thus far located is in 1796, eight years after Gainsborough's death. On December 15, 1796 (as already mentioned) Joseph Farington, after attending a sale of the possessions of Jonathan Buttall, noted that the picture was sold for 35 guineas. Within two years the fame of "The Blue Boy" seems to have been well established. In 1798 William Jackson, in the same essay on Gainsborough referred to earlier, states:

"Perhaps, his best portrait is that known among the painters by the name of the Blue-boy — it was in the possession of Mr. Buttall, near Newport-market." It is Farington once again, in another entry in his diary, dated May 25, 1802, who supplies some further history of the picture: "I painted till four o'clock & then went to Nesbitts sale in Grafton-street, where I met Hoppner who had purchased the Boy in Blue dress by Gainsborough which was Buthalls [sic] for 65 guineas. At Buthalls sale it was sold for 35 to Mr. Nesbitt." John Hoppner, himself a distinguished portraitist, had the painting for several years; at least Edward Edwards speaks of it in 1806 as still in his possession. But sometime before his death in 1810 he had disposed of it to his friend and patron, Robert, 2nd Earl Grosvenor, later 1st Marquis of Westminster. The portrait remained in the Westminster collection through the nineteenth century and until it was acquired in 1921 by Henry E. Huntington from Hugh, 2nd Duke of Westminster.

During the nineteenth century the fame of the painting became ever more widely and firmly established through its appearances at national and international exhibitions: at the British Institution in 1814 and 1834; at the Manchester Exhibition of 1857; at the International Exhibition, London, in 1862 and the Royal Academy in 1870; at the Grosvenor Gallery in 1885 and again at the Royal Academy in 1896; and at the Old English Masters Exhibition, Berlin, and the Franco-British Exhibition, London, both during 1908. By the early twentieth century "The Blue Boy" had become one of the most familiar and popular of all paintings. And this fame was even further augmented by the widely publicized circumstances surrounding the purchase of the picture by Mr. Huntington.

By 1921 Mr. Huntington was already well started on the formation of his great collection of British portraits. Several paintings of distinction, including Gainsborough's great portraits of Lord and Lady Ligonier, had been in his possession for a decade. The story attributed to the art dealer Joseph Duveen to the effect that Mr. Huntington first encountered a reproduction of "The Blue Boy" on the *Aquitania* in the summer of 1921 is untrue. We know that he owned a print of the painting as early as 1901. It seems more probable that Duveen, who accompanied Mr. and Mrs. Huntington on the voyage, knowing very well of their interest in British painting, and knowing also that the Duke of Westminster at that time was inclined to part with some of his treasures, simply put two and two together. In any event the sale was completed by an exchange of letters on October 7, 1921, between Mr. Huntington, then at Beauregard, near Versailles, and Duveen, then at his Paris office in the Place Vendôme.

Before the painting left England it was carefully cleaned and was exhibited at the National Gallery from January 4 until January 24, 1922. The cleaning was undertaken by William Holder, a London restorer, who had received many commissions to work on pictures in the National Gallery. The operation proceeded with the knowledge and support of Sir Charles Holmes, then Director of the National Gallery, and the Keeper, C. H. Collins Baker. The paint surface was found to be completely intact, and no retouchings were necessary. But the color relationships within the painting were radically changed when the heavy discolored layer of varnish was removed.

Judging from the newspaper reports, the public reaction to the transformation in the appearance of the painting was mixed, although generally favorable. Everyone was impressed by the fresh and brilliant color and the change in the hue of the costume from a rather murky green to an azure blue. Writers for *The Times* (December 31, 1921), *The Queen* (January 14, 1922), and the *Evening Standard* (January 16) all felt the change restored the painting to something like the appearance it must have had in the artist's own day. But there were others, notably in the *Morning Post* (January 3), who felt that the removal of the old varnish deprived the painting of some of its fascination: "Aloofness that was half its charm has disappeared with the old varnish. The figure now asserts itself, seems to have come out in front of the frame, and the illusion of height has gone."

At the close of the London showing, Sir Charles Holmes wrote to Duveen: "I saw the last, for the time being anyhow, of 'The Blue Boy' this afternoon at ten minutes past four, and feel bound to write these lines to thank you & Mr. Huntington for the pleasure which the sight of it has given to more than 90,000 people during the last three weeks. It is, indeed, a most brilliant thing, outshining in its present condition all our English pictures at Trafalgar Square, and when the natural mellowing of the varnish during the next two or three years has taken place its perfections will be enhanced."

The painting left England by a slightly circuitous route, arriving in New York on February 7, 1922. In an unusually informative letter Duveen outlined to Mr. Huntington the procedure followed. "One of our representatives who brought the picture over, tells me of an incident which I think will afford you much amusement. It appears that the Cunard Steamship Co. and the White Star Line have been for weeks angling for the shipment of the picture. Every time these two companies in London noticed any reference to the shipment of the Blue Boy, they either telephoned or called, anxious to have the honor of shipping it. I would like to say that attached to this honor was a small matter of the freight charge of one percent ad valorem . . . so their interest was not entirely disinterested. I can appreciate their disappointment when they learned, as they no doubt have done by this time, that I had it sent over by hand from France by the French Steamship Line, who imposed no freight charge at all upon objects coming by hand, beyond the usual excess baggage rate, which in this case amounted to not more than $200. or $300. There was undoubtedly a tremendous amount of competition amongst the shipping companies, whose representatives were on the qui-vive to find out how the case was actually going, but our man took it from London early one morning in a covered motor van by a circuitous route to Southampton, arriving at that port about 11 o'clock at night after all the shipping companies were closed. The case was then placed upon the S.S. Antonia, which plies between Southampton and Havre, at which latter port it arrived early Friday morning, and after going through the usual customs formalities, it was safely placed aboard the La Savoie. All through these arrangements the whole matter was kept a dead secret, and no one but our representative was aware of the shipment of the picture. The only person who probably became aware of its identity was the purser of the La Savoie during the last two or three days of the trip."

After the painting's arrival in New York it was exhibited at the Duveen Galleries from February 14 to March 7. On March 1 Duveen again wrote to Mr. Huntington, indicating that he expected to leave New York by train on March 17 bringing the painting to California, together with Gainsborough's "Cottage Door" and Sir Joshua Reynolds' great portrait of Mrs. Siddons as the Tragic Muse, both of which Mr. Huntington also purchased from the Duke of Westminster. "The Blue Boy" actually arrived in San Marino on Tuesday, March 21, 1922.

The painting hung at first in the large drawing room of the Huntington residence. With the completion of the Main Gallery in 1934 it was moved to these more spacious quarters, where (with the exception of the years during World War II) it has remained ever since. The visitor now meets the painting surrounded by one of the most distinguished collections of major British portraits to be found under one roof. "The Blue Boy" looks across the gallery to his almost equally famous, younger compatriot "Pinkie," painted by Sir Thomas Lawrence, while Reynolds' majestic portrait of Mrs. Siddons commands the space between. It is a compatible assembly in a sympathetic setting. Mr. Huntington's intention was to provide the paintings with an environment which was at least reminiscent of that for which they were originally intended. Thus the portraits are enhanced by eighteenth-century furnishings in rooms whose proportions and decorations derive from eighteenth-century prototypes. The pictures also hang as the painters intended they should: above eye level, where they form part of the decorative ensemble of the rooms. Certainly it is in this way that British portraits of the Georgian period appear to the greatest advantage. Divorced from such a setting and displayed in an impersonal atmosphere they lose a considerable portion of their appeal. And so "The Blue Boy," although far removed physically from its original home, has found another in which the painting must recognize much that is congenial and familiar, and where its popularity continues unabated.

Fig. 33. Sir Joshua Reynolds, *Mrs. Siddons as the Tragic Muse*, canvas, 93 x 57½ ins.

Chapter IV

Reynolds' "Mrs. Siddons as the Tragic Muse"

Sir Thomas Lawrence, speaking of "Mrs. Siddons as the Tragic Muse," called it "indisputably the finest female portrait in the world."[1] Nor was this a chance remark. At the time he made it, Lawrence was addressing his assembled colleagues and the students at the Royal Academy. It was the occasion of the annual distribution of prizes on December 10, 1823. Lawrence had been elected president of the Academy more than three years earlier, but this was the first time he had given a formal lecture. It was, in this sense, his inaugural address, a serious moment when he would have considered his words carefully.

Sir Thomas was not alone in his superlative praise of Sir Joshua Reynolds' portrait of Mrs. Siddons. Many years earlier the professor of painting at the Royal Academy, a hot-tempered Irishman by the name of James Barry (who was no particular friend of Reynolds), referred to "The Tragic Muse" as "the finest picture of the kind, perhaps in the world."[2]

Much as one admires the painting today, and it certainly is one of the grandest of British portraits, the praise given it by Barry and Lawrence strikes the modern ear as extravagant and rather puzzling. It would seem that their criteria for judging a portrait were different from ours and that they saw values in the painting which are less apparent to twentieth-century eyes. We cannot now hope to recover a full, sympathetic awareness of the basis on which they made their judgment — nearly two centuries of changing tastes make that impossible — but it is profitable to explore some of the considerations that led these perceptive critics to place the painting on such a lofty pedestal.

For anyone coming to the painting with a fresh eye and no knowledge of the personalities and circumstances involved, the first impression must surely be one of dignity and solemnity. It is an impression created not only by the pose and bearing of the central figure herself, and her costume, but also by the attitudes of her two shadowy attendants, by the arrangement of the figures, and by the color. The color, especially in relation to that of the other portraits in the Huntington Gallery, must appear as one of the most remarkable features of the painting. To the casual glance the picture seems monochromatic. The dominant tone is a rich golden brown, interrupted only by the creamy areas of the face and arms and by the deep velvety shadows of the background. On closer examination a much greater variety in the color is apparent, but the first impression remains valid for the painting as a unit.

The central figure sits on a thronelike chair. She does not look at the spectator but appears in deep contemplation; her expression is one of melancholy musing. Her gestures aptly reinforce the meditative air of the head and also contribute to the regal quality of the whole figure. A great pendent cluster of pearls adorns the front of her dress. In the heavy, sweeping draperies that envelop the figure there are no frivolous elements of feminine costume to conflict with the initial effect of solemn grandeur.

In the background, dimly seen on either side of the throne, are two attendant figures. One, with lowered head and melancholy expression, holds a bloody dagger; the other, his features contorted into an expression of horror, grasps a cup. Surely these figures speak of dire and violent events. Their presence adds a sinister impression to a picture already heavily charged with grave qualities.

The artist has carefully arranged the figures and other elements of the picture to create an effect of balance and stability. Pyramidal shapes within the central figure are enframed by the sides of the throne and the two shadowy attendants. The symmetry of the grouping contributes to the air of solemnity. The deliberations of the artist are also apparent in such details as the placement of the dagger and the cup in relation to the right and left hands of the principal figure. From whatever standpoint one examines the painting, it constantly yields evidence of the thoughtful and thoroughly consistent manner in which the artist has worked; nowhere is there a jarring note at odds with the general impression.

But effective as the painting undoubtedly is in simple visual terms, one feels that Lawrence and Barry must have had more than this in mind when they praised the picture so highly. And indeed it is not until one places the painting in its historical context and attempts to understand the circumstances governing its creation that it begins to attain its full dimensions as a work of art.

First among the factors are the two principal personalities involved: Mrs. Siddons and Sir Joshua Reynolds, certainly two of the most commanding figures of their day. At the time the portrait was painted, Sarah Siddons was in her late twenties, but she already had a solid decade of acting experience behind her. She was born in 1755, the daughter of Roger Kemble, manager of an itinerant company of actors. Most of her early acting experience was with her father's company touring through English provincial centers. Her reputation rose so quickly that in 1775, when she was only twenty, she was engaged by Garrick to perform at Drury Lane. But this early London adventure proved premature; she was unsuccessful and retired again to the provincial circuits, acting princi-

pally at Bath. She threw her full energies into building her repertory and per-
fecting her acting technique, with the result that her return to London as a
tragic actress in the autumn of 1782 was one of the great sensations of theater
history. The audience and the critics gave her tumultuous acclaim. Almost
overnight she found herself the unquestioned first lady of the British stage, a
position she retained for thirty years.

The reputation she enjoyed was distinctly different from that of a mid
twentieth-century theatrical star. The leading intellectuals and statesmen of
the day were among her most fervent admirers and were in constant attendance
at her performances. Mrs. Siddons herself in her memoirs (as quoted by Thomas
Campbell) speaks of the reception her acting received from these notables: "O
glorious constellation! Burke, Gibbon, Sheridan, Windham, and, though last,
not least, the illustrious Fox, of whom it was frequently said, that iron tears were
drawn down Pluto's gloomy cheeks. And these great men would often visit my
dressing-room, after the play, to make their bows and honour me with their
applauses. I must repeat, O glorious days! Neither did his royal highness the
Prince of Wales withhold this testimony of his approbation." George III and
Queen Charlotte were so impressed that, although they did not normally care
much for tragedy, they came to see Mrs. Siddons in all her roles, and she was
given an official court appointment as Preceptress in English Reading to the
Princesses.

Among the intelligentsia who flocked to see the great actress and returned
again and again was Sir Joshua Reynolds, the august president of the Royal
Academy. In that first triumphant London season of Mrs. Siddons, Reynolds
was in his late fifties. He was at the time the most respected painter in England,
and he also enjoyed a wide reputation as a theorist and writer on art, based on
the discourses or lectures he delivered from time to time to his colleagues and
the students in the Royal Academy.

Reynolds moved with ease among the great men of his day. Samuel Johnson
and Edmund Burke were his close friends. Mrs. Siddons remarks in her memoirs:
"I had frequently the honour of dining with Sir Joshua Reynolds, in Leicester
Square. At his house were assembled all the good, the wise, the talented, the rank
and fashion of the age." But Reynolds was not in the best of health. He had suf-
fered a paralytic stroke late in 1782, from which he probably did not fully
recover. His hearing, always bad, was deteriorating. Before the end of the decade
his sight was so seriously impaired that he was obliged to set aside his brush. He
sent fewer paintings than usual to the Royal Academy exhibition early in 1783,
and they were not particularly well received. Horace Walpole noted at the
time: "Poor Sir Joshua seems to decline since his illness." Possibly it was to
counteract this impression and to prove to himself that his powers were not
failing that Reynolds put forth a particularly strong effort during 1783 and
early 1784. He sent no less than seventeen paintings to the Royal Academy

exhibition in the spring of the latter year (with one exception the largest number he ever exhibited), and included among the pictures was the portrait generally considered by his contemporaries to be his masterpiece, now known as "Mrs. Siddons as the Tragic Muse."

There are many details concerning Reynolds' creation of the portrait of Mrs. Siddons that are not recorded, but we know most of the general facts about the origin of the picture. Although it was not exhibited until April 1784, it is clear from Reynolds' letters that he had started working on it a full year before, at least as early as the first week of May 1783. Unfortunately, Reynolds' sitter book for 1783 is missing, so the precise date when the portrait was begun is unknown.

A great deal of ink has been spilled concerning the selection of the pose of Mrs. Siddons. From many anecdotes that have survived, it is clear the lady felt that she herself had determined it. In one account, preserved in her memoirs, she says of Reynolds and the portrait: "When I attended him for the first sitting, after more gratifying encomiums than I can now repeat, he took me by the hand, saying, 'Ascend your undisputed throne, and graciously bestow upon me some good idea of the Tragic Muse.' I walked up the steps, and instantly seated myself in the attitude in which the Tragic Muse now appears. This idea satisfied him so well, that without one moment's hesitation he determined not to alter it."

According to Samuel Rogers, the choice was more accidental than Mrs. Siddons' own account would suggest. He told Mrs. Siddons' biographer, Thomas Campbell, "I was at Sir Joshua's studio when Mrs. Siddons came in, having walked rapidly to be in time for her appointment. She threw herself, out of breath, into an armchair; having taken off her bonnet and dropped her head upon her left hand — the other hand drooping over the arm of the chair. Suddenly lifting her head she said, 'How shall I sit?' 'Just as you are,' said Sir Joshua, and so she is painted."[3]

But it is clear enough from the visual evidence of the picture itself that if Mrs. Siddons in some way suggested the pose (and Sir Joshua was far too much of a gentleman to contradict her) this suggestion could have been no more than a hint from which Reynolds' inventive genius evolved the final product. The painting is in fact a brilliantly successful synthesis of images and ideas from a wide variety of sources.

The basic notion of representing Mrs. Siddons in the guise of the Tragic Muse may well have been suggested to Reynolds by a poem honoring the actress written by William Russell and published early in 1783, just a few weeks prior to the time the painting was probably begun. The title is *The Tragic Muse: A Poem Addressed to Mrs. Siddons.* The verses themselves are not distinguished, but the title and the poet's initial image of Mrs. Siddons enthroned as Melpomene, the muse of tragedy, may have lodged in Reynolds' memory and given an initial direction to his thinking about the portrait.

It has long been recognized that in the basic organization of the picture Reynolds had Michelangelo's prophets and sybils of the Sistine ceiling in mind. Mrs. Siddons' pose (the lady's own comments notwithstanding) recalls that of Isaiah, and of the two attendant figures the one on the left of the picture is very closely modeled on the similarly placed companion of the prophet Jeremiah (*Figs. 34 and 35*).

Reynolds must have intended the informed spectator to make this connection. Lawrence, of course, recognized it and mentioned it in his comments on the painting in 1823. Mrs. Siddons' early biographer, James Boaden, speaks of it in his 1827 memoir. But one is left with the curious fact that apparently the lady herself was unaware of the relationship.

Reynolds' attitude toward this sort of borrowing from the work of other artists may seem a little strange to us today. He recognized two rather distinct uses that a painter might make of the work of the masters. He thought, as did most of his contemporaries, that great works of art should serve as a school for aspiring painters. The point is taken up in one of his Discourses to the students at the Royal Academy: "He, who borrows an idea from an antient, or even from a modern artist not his contemporary, and so accommodates it to his own work, that it makes a part of it, with no seam or joining appearing, can hardly be charged with plagiarism: poets practise this kind of borrowing, without reserve.

ig. 34. Michelangelo, *Jeremiah*, from the Sistine eiling, fresco (Anderson Art Reference Bureau).

Fig. 35. Michelangelo, *Isaiah*, from the Sistine ceiling, fresco (Anderson Art Reference Bureau).

But an artist should not be contented with this only; he should enter into a competition with his original, and endeavour to improve what he is appropriating to his own work. Such imitation is so far from having any thing in it of the servility of plagiarism, that it is a perpetual exercise of the mind, a continual invention. Borrowing or stealing with such art and caution, will have a right to the same lenity as was used by the Lacedemonians; who did not punish theft, but the want of artifice to conceal it." From this point of view "The Tragic Muse" is a perfect illustration of Reynolds' advice to the student. The basic connection is certainly there; but at every point Reynolds has modified, adapted, and transformed his model in accordance with his own controlling idea. Yet the new composition has complete coherence, "with no seam or joining appearing."

But Reynolds also realized that borrowing from the works of earlier masters could be put to a more subtle use. He understood that association and suggestion can be important factors in our reactions to a work of art; that a great deal depends on what has become familiar and on what we have come to like and admire. He discusses the matter in a well-known passage from one of his Discourses (quoted above, p. 8) in which he considers the use of the Van Dyck habit in mid-eighteenth-century English portraits. One might add that in spite of Reynolds' somewhat superior tone in this passage he used the Van Dyck habit in his own paintings more than did any other major portraitist and continued to do so for several years after he delivered the lecture from which the passage was quoted. Indeed there can be little doubt that Reynolds frequently sought to enrich the appeal of his own painting by this sort of allusion to or quotation from the works of earlier masters. Thus he expected that by associating "The Tragic Muse" with Michelangelo in the mind of the spectator he could attach to it some tincture of the awe and respect with which Michelangelo's work is regarded.

If the arrangement of the figures in the portrait of Mrs. Siddons suggests Michelangelo, other aspects of the painting, particularly the color, the heavy shadow effects, and the actual application of the paint, have nothing to do with the Italian master. The Sistine ceiling is, of course, executed in fresco; the colors are comparatively light, the surface is smooth, and the forms seldom lose themselves in the deep enveloping shadows with which Reynolds surrounds Mrs. Siddons. The rather thick buttery pigment that Reynolds uses and the rich golden brown tonality of the whole painting are totally unlike the work of Michelangelo and suggest instead the paintings of Rembrandt. Of course Reynolds knew the works of Rembrandt, and he had fine examples, including the so-called "Man in Armour," in his own collection. He recognized Rembrandt's particular skill in the depiction of special light effects by means of which he could generate a sense of mystery and drama. Although Rembrandt was not an artist for whom Reynolds expressed any deep sympathy, there can be no doubt that some of his most searching self-portraits were inspired by the Dutch master. It is probable Reynolds realized that the air of melancholy foreboding with which he wished to surround the image of "The Tragic Muse" could be developed with the aid of a rich Rembrandtesque chiaroscuro.

There are still further visual recollections and images that must have occupied Reynolds' mind as he designed his great portrait, particularly when he came to deal with the two shadowy attendants behind Mrs. Siddons' throne. If the basic idea of placing two figures in that position came from Michelangelo, the problem of fitting the figures into Reynolds' particular conception led him to draw upon still other sources.

The two figures constitute an interesting puzzle connected with the painting, primarily because some uncertainty has arisen about the way in which they should be interpreted. The explanation that has found widest acceptance is that they represent Crime and Remorse. This is the view taken by C. H. Collins Baker in the careful catalog he made of the paintings in the Huntington collection some thirty years ago, and it has been followed by most students ever since. According to this interpretation, the dagger carried by the figure to Mrs. Siddons' right would symbolize Crime, the cup carried by the figure to her left, Remorse or Sorrow. This suggestion fits well enough with our general reaction to the picture. Yet investigation quickly reveals another possible interpretation which rests in fact on a much firmer foundation.

Aristotle, in a famous passage in the *Poetics*, defined tragedy as "an imitation, in ornamental language, of an action important and complete, and possessing a certain degree of magnitude, having its forms distinct in their respective parts, and by the representation of persons acting, and not by narration, effecting through the means of pity and terror, the purgation of such passions." This definition was, of course, very well known in the eighteenth century. It had been quoted, analyzed, discussed for hundreds of years whenever the question of defining tragedy arose. Reynolds must have known the passage well, and it is likely that he heard his learned literary friends expatiate on the matter more than once. Indeed the passage was so familiar that one suspects an eighteenth-century audience viewing a painting that involved a personification of tragedy with two companions would at once assume that the companions were Pity and Terror. This is precisely how the early biographer of Mrs. Siddons, James Boaden, interpreted the attendant figures. Boaden's book appeared in 1827, while Mrs. Siddons was still alive. He was a careful scholar, widely connected in London literary and theatrical circles, whose remarks on the painting must carry the authority of a near-contemporary source.

The Crime and Remorse interpretation does not seem to have appeared until the middle of the nineteenth century, when Tom Taylor in a footnote to his useful but none-too-reliable study of Reynolds speaks of the attendant figures: "Called by some Pity and Terror, by others Pity and Remorse, but more like Crime and Remorse." Taylor seems to have had no textual or other justification for his interpretation, and it is curious that it should in subsequent studies of the painting have so largely superseded the earlier and much more probable explanation.

There is one additional bit of evidence that can be brought to bear on the problem, and it weighs heavily in favor of Pity and Terror. This evidence brings us back again to the visual images and recollections coursing through Reynolds' mind when he composed the painting.

The French seventeenth-century artist Charles Le Brun wrote a curious but popular and influential treatise on the passions. Le Brun suggested that the various emotional states or passions took specific form in the human face. His book was intended as a sort of manual from which painters could derive the proper facial expression to convey any particular passion. Le Brun went so far as to illustrate his book with engravings showing the different expressions. The treatise was translated into English in 1734, accompanied by the diagrams. Although the specific names "pity" and "terror" do not occur among the passions illustrated, "compassion" and "fright" do. A comparison of these with the heads of Reynolds' two attendant figures in "The Tragic Muse" is most interesting. The similarities seem rather too close to be accidental (*Figs. 36 and 37*).

There is a drawing in the Tate Gallery that is considered to be a self-portrait study for the figure of Terror. If this identification is correct, then the drawing indicates that Reynolds tested Le Brun against experience. But the position of

Figs. 36 and 37. Charles LeBrun, *Compassion* and *Fright*, from *Method to Learn to Design the Passions*, trans. John Williams (London 1734).

Fig. 38. Cesare Ripa, *Melpomene*, from
Iconologia, trans. George Richardson
(London 1779).

the head, the treatment of the hair, and the general configuration serve only to
confirm still further that Reynolds had Le Brun's diagrams in mind. It would
seem that we are here confronted with yet another instance of Reynolds' visual
borrowing. Once again one is impressed by how smoothly the images are woven
into the whole fabric and how effortlessly they take their places in the general
Michelangelesque composition.

But in dealing with the two attendants we are still left with the dagger and
the cup. What have these two objects to do with Pity and Terror? It was surely
this discrepancy that led to the theory that the figures stood for Crime and
Remorse. The dagger and cup, however, are the normal attributes of Melpomene, the muse of tragedy, and they are the means by which this figure is properly identified in pictorial representations. The great source of information
about this sort of problem is the *Iconologia* of Cesare Ripa, a book that was well
known to Reynolds. In an English version prepared by George Richardson and
published in 1779 the reader is told that Melpomene "is painted in a grave
aspect, in an heroick dress, with her head finely attired; she holds a cup in one
hand, and a dagger in the other, with a crown and scepter at her feet; she is shod
in buskins, which were used by the ancient tragedians . . ." The dagger and cup
then are normal attributes of Melpomene; they relate to the central figure of the
muse herself rather than to her attendants (*Fig. 38*).

Specifically what the dagger and cup signify in connection with Melpomene isn't quite so clear. Richardson says "they allude to the happiness or misery incident to human life," which is pretty vague. Boaden understood the bloody dagger and cup of poison to symbolize the most frequent forms of violent death in tragedy. Once again, Boaden's proximity to the persons and circumstances surrounding the creation of the painting entitles his opinion to careful consideration.

The roster of Reynolds' sources in the creation of "The Tragic Muse" begins to sound rather formidable: Michelangelo, Rembrandt, Le Brun, Ripa. But the amazing thing is that the finished product is in no sense a pastiche. These disparate elements have all been transformed in the passage through Reynolds' own visual imagination and have emerged as a unit in which the relationship of all the parts to one another seems not only correct but inevitable. This in itself is an achievement commanding our admiration, but we cannot fully appreciate the significance of this achievement for Reynolds and his contemporaries unless at the same time we understand something of their theory of art: what they considered art should be and attempt to do.

Reynolds felt that the fundamental purpose of art was ethical and moral. Its aim was to elevate the thoughts of the spectator, to purge his mind of petty and mean considerations through the "contemplation of universal rectitude and harmony." The greatest art, accordingly, dealt with lofty themes of human and divine achievement. Furthermore, it employed a lofty style or manner in presenting these themes that corresponded with the character of the subject. The accidents of nature, whether in the human figure or in the setting, were ironed away; the temporal and changing in matters of dress and fashion were eliminated; the frivolous and decorative aspects of painting (especially where colors and textures were involved) were submerged in a desire for grandeur and solemnity.

These were the ideas Reynolds supported and expounded in his lectures, and there was nothing unusual about them. This was the attitude toward art held by most intelligent and informed men of the day, and it had been the dominant point of view of European art theorists for the preceding three hundred years. But it is rather different from most twentieth-century theories which tend to regard the function of art as heightening and extending sensation rather than promoting morality and virtue.

Granting the general conception held by Reynolds and his contemporaries concerning the purpose of painting, it is clear that they could not assign a high value to portraiture, for the portraitist dealt in precisely those particularities and eccentricities of individual appearance that were incompatible with both the lofty subject matter and the style considered essential for great art. But Reynolds felt it might be possible, when the occasion warranted it, for the portraitist to borrow from the grand manner of painting: "If a portrait-painter is desirous to raise and improve his subject, he has no other means than by approaching it to a general idea. He leaves out all the minute breaks and peculiarities in the face, and changes the dress from a temporary fashion to one more permanent, which has annexed to it no ideas of meanness from its being familiar to us." This procedure is exactly the one Reynolds is following in "The Tragic Muse," and the great fascination of the portrait for his contemporaries lay in the success with which he was able to elevate the whole expressive character of the painting to the point where it partook of the grand style. This is the basic purpose behind the allusions to Michelangelo and behind the generalized dress which Mrs. Siddons wears. Even in the depiction of the fabric Reynolds follows his own advice to students: "It is the inferior stile that marks the variety of stuffs. With him [the painter of the grand style], the cloathing is neither woollen, nor linen, nor silk, sattin, or velvet: it is drapery; it is nothing more." And so it is that the great folds of fabric enveloping Mrs. Siddons do not reveal themselves as anything more than a heavy and substantial material. Likewise in the matter of color Reynolds advises the student: "To give a general air of grandeur at first view, all trifling or artful play of little lights, or an attention to a variety of tints is to be avoided; a quietness and simplicity must reign over the whole work; to which a breadth of uniform, and simple colour, will very much contribute." And thus it is with "The Tragic Muse."

If one doubts the extent to which Reynolds deliberately adjusted his means to the end in view when painting "The Tragic Muse," it is necessary only to compare the picture with another he executed at the same time in which he is aiming for a different type of effect. The portrait of Lavinia, Countess Spencer, and her son Viscount Althorp (also in the Huntington collection) is a charming depiction of maternal affection. The little boy, one supposes, has bumped his head, and his mother comforts him, kneeling by his side. The arrangement of the two figures and the draperies have been beautifully worked out to create for the eye a more or less circular path that envelops the mother and child and emphasizes the nature of their relationship. Reynolds is here aiming for a general effect of warmth and intimacy with a touch of sentiment; there is nothing of the solemn and lofty tone he wanted in "The Tragic Muse." All of the specific and temporal details that he deliberately eliminated in the portrait of Mrs. Siddons are here clearly in evidence and make an important contribution to the effect of the painting. The color is much lighter in key, with considerable variety in tints; the dress, the hat, the coiffure are all those of a fashionable woman of the day; and Reynolds seems to have taken positive delight in differentiating the textures of the various fabrics; the setting is an English park such as the Countess might very well frequent (*Fig. 39*).

When one sees the two paintings beside one another, there can be no doubt that all Reynolds' adjustments in "The Tragic Muse" were quite conscious and deliberate in an effort to elevate the general effect of the painting toward the

Fig. 39. Sir Joshua Reynolds, *Lavinia, Countess Spencer and Viscount Althorp,* canvas, 57½ x 43 ins.

Fig. 41. Sir Joshua Reynolds, *Duchess of Hamilton,* canvas, 93 x 57 ins. (The Lady Lever Gallery, Port Sunlight).

Fig. 40. Sir Joshua Reynolds, *Countess of Albemarle,* canvas, 49¾ x 39¾ ins. (The National Gallery, London).

grand style that he and his contemporaries admired so much. And it was primarily his brilliant success in achieving this end, through means we have already discussed, that so impressed men like Barry and Lawrence. "Mrs. Siddons as the Tragic Muse" is in fact one of the very few portraits that attain the air of nobility of the grand style. It transcends what Reynolds and his contemporaries considered the normal limits of portraiture and rises to a type of expression thought to be the prerogative of great narrative paintings. In this sense it is an amazing achievement, and it is primarily in this sense that Lawrence referred to it as "indisputably the finest female portrait in the world."

But if the portrait of Mrs. Siddons emphasizes Reynolds' connection with earlier traditions and outlooks, the fact that he could change his approach radically when painting a portrait of a different type (such as Lady Spencer and her son) is characteristic of his own age. His wish to command a wide range of expression, and his willingness and ability to make extensive adjustments in his manner of painting to achieve this end both exemplify the late eighteenth-century, early romantic point of view. Reynolds developed this control early in his career, and some of the most dramatic instances of his ability to alter his approach come from the late 1750's. The direct, empirical manner in the Countess of Albemarle (*Fig. 40*), for instance, where the lady is presented in her normal clothes, engaged in the homely task of knotting wool, is in startling contrast to the contemporary portrait of the Duchess of Hamilton (*Fig. 41*), where the whole picture is a highly sophisticated concoction of learned allusions.

Reynolds was justifiably proud of his portrait of Mrs. Siddons. But as frequently happens when we know we have a good thing, it was difficult for him to leave it alone. He must have been fussing with the picture for the better part of a year. At least one prominent artist, Gilbert Stuart, who saw the painting at an early and then at a much later stage, thought that Reynolds diluted the power of his performance by working over the picture. Mrs. Siddons herself tells an interesting anecdote about the last stages in the completion of the portrait: "When I attended him for the last sitting, he seemed to be afraid of touching the picture; and after pausingly contemplating his work, he said 'No, I will merely add a little more colour to the face.' I then begged him to pardon my presumption in hoping that he would not heighten that tone of complexion so deeply accordant with the chilly and concentrated musings of pale melancholy. He most graciously complied with my petition; and, some time afterward, when he invited me to go and see the picture finished, and in the frame, he did me the honour to thank me for persuading him to pause from heightening the colour, being now perfectly convinced that it would have impaired the effect: adding, that he had been inexpressibly gratified by observing many persons strongly affected in contemplating this favourite effort of his pencil. I was delighted when he assured me that he was certain the colours would remain unfaded as long as the canvass would keep them together, which, unhappily, has not been

Fig. 42. Francis Haward, after Reynolds, *Mrs. Siddons as the Tragic Muse*, (detail, showing form of the signature on the hem of the dress), stipple engraving.

the case with all his works: he gallantly added, with his benevolent smile, 'And, to confirm my opinion, here is my name; for I have resolved to go down to posterity on the hem of your garment.' "

Reynolds did in fact sign and date the picture, presenting his name as an embroidery on the skirt. It is a practice he is known to have used in only one other portrait, in itself eloquent testimony of the esteem in which he held the painting. The signature has almost disappeared in the original, but its form is preserved for us in the engraving made by Francis Haward in 1787 (*Fig. 42*).

On the whole, Reynolds was justified in telling Mrs. Siddons that the colors would not fade. The overall tonality of the painting must be somewhat darker than it was originally, and parts of it have become obscure, but the general impression has probably changed very little. It was always a somber picture. But if the colors may not have altered radically, there is at least one feature of Reynolds' technical procedure in the painting that has had a serious effect on its appearance. Reynolds was constantly experimenting with pigments and media. He discovered that a beautiful, warm, dark, velvety tone could be produced by the use of bitumen. Bitumen or asphaltum is a tarlike substance. When used as underpainting 'in a picture (as Reynolds has used it in the dark background areas of "The Tragic Muse"), it never really hardens but continues to flow slightly, opening up broad, deep cracks in the layers of paint. This condition is very marked in the background areas of "The Tragic Muse" but fortunately is practically absent from the figure itself.

The history of the painting subsequent to its sensational debut in 1784 is fairly clear and uncomplicated. Reynolds did not paint the picture on commission but primarily (one must assume) for his own satisfaction and as an object for public exhibition. He placed the very high price of 1,000 guineas on it (his normal price for a full-length portrait at the time was 200 guineas). As a result, the painting remained with the artist until 1790, by which time Reynolds was virtually blind. It was then purchased by C. A. de Calonne, through the dealer Desenfans, for £735. De Calonne, who had been minister of finance to Louis XVI, had fled to

England in 1787. When his collection was sold in 1795, the painting was purchased by William Smith, member of Parliament for Norwich, for £336. Smith sold the picture privately to another member of Parliament, G. Watson Taylor, for £900, and in Taylor's sale at Christie's on June 13, 1823, it was purchased by Robert, second Earl Grosvenor, later first Marquis of Westminster, for £1,837. The painting remained in the Westminster collection through the nineteenth century. It was offered for sale, but not in fact sold, at Christie's July 4, 1919. The painting was purchased by Henry E. Huntington through Joseph Duveen in November 1921 and was paid for at the same time as "The Blue Boy," also acquired from the Duke of Westminster. Both paintings reached San Marino on March 21, 1922.

Reynolds painted a replica of the portrait in about 1789, which is now in Dulwich College. The facts that this painting also passed into the hands of the dealer Desenfans and that it left Reynolds' studio at just about the same time as the first version have given grounds for some confusion between the two. Fortunately, however, the Dulwich version is clearly dated 1789, whereas that in the Huntington collection is dated 1784, so there can be no doubt concerning precedence. The question of whether or not the Dulwich version is entirely from Reynolds' own hand is fortunately one with which we need not here concern ourselves in detail. Reynolds certainly maintained studio assistants. Considering the artist's infirmities at the time the second version was executed, one is probably justified in assuming that much of it is the work of his helpers. But the fact that he was willing to have his name appear on it in the same form as on the first version argues that he at least gave close supervision to the second picture. The second version seems to contain even more bitumen than the first, with the result that its qualities are much obscured by its condition.

For many years after "The Tragic Muse" arrived in San Marino, the painting hung in the principal hall of the Huntington residence. When the Main Gallery addition was completed in 1934, it was transferred to this much larger space, which is better suited to the heroic character of the painting. It has always occupied the place of honor in the gallery, commanding a room that probably houses the most distinguished collection of British full-length portraits brought together in one spot. And if the thoughts of all the artists whose works hang in that gallery could be known, this arrangement would likely meet with their full approval. For in "The Tragic Muse" Reynolds achieved an air of grandeur and dignity which he and his contemporaries regarded as a prime objective of art and which no other portrait of the day embodied so successfully.

[1]D. E. Williams, ed., *The Life and Correspondence of Sir Thomas Lawrence* (London, 1831), I, p. 430.

[2]*The Works of James Barry, Esq.* (London, 1809), I, p. 553.

[3]William Whitley, *Artists & Their Friends in England 1700-1799* (London, 1928), II, 4.

Fig. 43. Sir Thomas Lawrence, *Pinkie*, canvas, 57½ x 39¼ ins.

Chapter V

Lawrence's "Pinkie"

"I BECOME every day more desirous to see my dear little Pinkey; but as I cannot gratify myself with the Original, I must beg the favor of You to have her picture drawn at full Length by one of the best Masters in an easy Careless attitude. As your Taste & Judg'ment cannot be excell'd, I leave her Dress to you. — You will therefore be so kind as to inform me by the first pacquet after you receive this, what the Amount will be, and I will get a Bill & send You as soon as possible. — I shall expect it out as soon as the paint is well dried & Seasoned — Let the frame be handsome & neat."[1]

This passage from a letter by an affectionate grandmother marks the origin of the painting now known the world over as "Pinkie." The author of the letter was Judith Barrett, and she wrote from St. James', Jamaica, on November 16, 1793.

The Barretts were a family of well-established landholders in Jamaica who had been associated with the island ever since the British conquest in 1655. During the following century and a half they had extended their holdings so that by the late eighteenth century they owned several important estates and were deeply involved in the sugar and rum production that were the controlling factors in the island's economy. The family fortunes were probably at their highest point in the 1790's.

Judith Barrett's daughter, Elizabeth, married a certain Charles Moulton in 1781; and Pinkie, Sarah Goodin Barrett Moulton, was their first child. She was born on one of the Barrett estates, Little River, St. James', Jamaica, on March 22, 1783. It was also on the Barrett estates, and particularly at a house called Cinnamon Hill, that Pinkie passed her early childhood and became (we may assume) a particular favorite with her grandmother. One can well imagine that Judith Barrett would have very mixed feelings when it was decided, probably in 1792, that Pinkie should accompany her two younger brothers, Edward and Samuel, to England, where the children were to be educated. The journey was a long one (six to eight weeks); the times were uncertain (England and France were at war by 1793); clearly it would be many years before Mrs. Barrett could expect to see her grandchildren again.

Mrs. Barrett had a niece, Elizabeth Barrett Williams, who lived near London on Richmond Hill. The children from Jamaica did not apparently stay with Mrs. Williams, but she was very much interested in their welfare, and it seems to have been through her that the doting Judith Barrett kept in touch with her grandchildren.

The letter asking for a portrait of Pinkie was received by Mrs. Williams on February 11, 1794. One does not particularly envy the lady the task appointed her. Commissioning a portrait for someone else is always a delicate and rather unsatisfactory business, and for an affectionate grandmother on the other side of the Atlantic must have been especially so. Furthermore, aside from the facts that the portrait was to be full-length and exhibit Pinkie in "an easy careless attitude," all the details were left up to Mrs. Williams, whose "taste and judgment" were thus to be put to the test.

The first problem, of course, was to settle on an artist. Half a dozen years earlier the choice of "one of the best masters" would almost certainly have fallen on Reynolds or Gainsborough. But Gainsborough had died in 1788, and Reynolds in 1792. The two real giants of British portraiture were both gone, but somewhat too recently gone for the line of succession to be clearly visible. George Romney was still painting, but his abilities were noticeably on the decline. Gilbert Stuart, full of a promising London career in the 1780's, was back in America by 1793. Mrs. Williams was thus obliged to turn to the younger men, of whom the most prominent at the time were John Hoppner, William Beechey, and (much the youngest of the three) Thomas Lawrence. To us today, with the hindsight offered by over a century and a half of distance, there can be no doubt that Lawrence was the best man. But the relative merits of the three could not have been so clear then, although something did occur just as Mrs. Williams received Mrs. Barrett's letter that may well have been decisive in steering her to Lawrence.

Lawrence at the time was approaching his twenty-fifth birthday. He had been something of a child prodigy, drawing portraits of the visitors at his father's coaching inn, "The Black Bear," at Devizes when he was ten. But he had fortunately been able to negotiate successfully the difficult transition from a boy wonder to an adult artist. His first great success came at the Royal Academy exhibition of 1790, where he showed full-length portraits of Queen Charlotte and the popular actress Elizabeth Farren, later Countess of Derby. The latter painting in particular (now in the Metropolitan Museum) was a lively and scintillating achievement that did a great deal to establish the young portraitist's reputation. He was elected an associate of the Academy in the next year, and following the death of Reynolds he was offered the post of Painter in Ordinary to the King. On February 10, 1794 (the day before the arrival of Mrs. Barrett's letter), Lawrence was elected a full academician, squeezing out Hoppner by two votes. This success must have appeared to give him clear priority in the estimation of his professional colleagues, and it was timed perfectly to help Mrs. Williams with her choice.

We know nothing in detail about the actual commissioning of the portrait. One naturally wonders how much Mrs. Williams may have had to do with matters such as costume and pose. It would be particularly interesting to learn whether young Miss Moulton's nickname had anything to do with the prominent use of pink. Of course the name "Pinkie" as applied to Sarah probably had no reference to color. The word simply means small or diminutive, and likely referred to the little girl's size rather than her rosy cheeks. Nevertheless it is both tempting and plausible to suppose that the nickname may have suggested the color.

The pose is also an interesting facet of the portrait. Mrs. Barrett asked for "an easy careless attitude," which certainly left a wide range of possibilities. But the actual pose chosen is a distinctive and unusual one. It is difficult to explain the position and gesture of the left arm and hand in relation to any particular action. The gesture is one Lawrence does not ever seem to have used again. Possibly Pinkie is caught in a little private dance that would have special meaning for her grandmother.

But whatever personal references may or may not be intended in such matters as the pose and color scheme, the total impact of the painting is distinctly in Lawrence's own idiom. As is often the case with works of art that enjoy great popularity and are extensively reproduced, the effect of the original painting on the spectator who sees it for the first time is almost startlingly vigorous and fresh. The reproductions and the context in which they frequently occur create a saccharine air about the picture which is at complete variance with the painting itself. The little girl's face is in fact firmly set, with no indication of a smile. The rather severe expression is accentuated by the completely frontal presentation of the face — a position for the head which Lawrence used often and which tends to give added force and directness to the relation between the sitter and the spectator.

Fig. 44. Sir Thomas Lawrence, *Pinkie*, (detail).

Fig. 45. Sir Thomas Lawrence, *Pinkie*, (detail).

The color scheme of the picture is on the cool side: deep greens in the landscape, a turbulent sky, and the white of the dress relieved only by the pink of the sash and ribbons and of the little girl's complexion. The brisk, fresh quality of the painting is greatly enhanced by the breeze blowing the dress and ribbons, and by the low horizon line, which gives the impression that Pinkie is standing on the crest of a hill. Lawrence's early brushwork is in complete harmony with the other expressive qualities of the picture. His paint application at this time has been aptly described as "waxy, crisp, and scintillating." There is a freedom and bravura in the way the paint goes on that accords perfectly with the mood of the portrait.

The spirited, lively presentation of the figure employed by Lawrence follows a tradition established by Reynolds, who frequently animated a woman's portrait by depicting the sitter stepping forth across a lawn with a breeze rippling through her gown and hair. But aside from this general idea, Lawrence does not seem to have had any particular model in mind for "Pinkie"; the details of the pose and composition are his own. The painting, when it first appeared, would have seemed remarkably unhackneyed in all respects, a bright indication of the originality of the rising young star in British portraiture.

Work on the portrait must have proceeded without much delay after Mrs. Williams received her aunt's letter in February of 1794. On September 1 of that year Mrs. Williams sent a progress report to Mrs. Barrett. We do not have the actual letter, but it is clear from Mrs. Barrett's reply that the portrait must have been well along, although not finished: "I am exceedingly obliged to You for the trouble You have taken about the picture and shall Consider myself indebted still farther, if You will be so obliging as to have it well packed when it is ready to be Ship'd. I observe what You say respecting the frame — and I think the best way will be, for You to send me an exact account of what I shall owe You after the frame and any other expences are paid for and I will remit You immediately the balance — for by sending 12 Guineas more it wou'd pay for the frame, but some other Expence might be incur'd, & I shou'd still have to remit to You again.

"I am really happy to hear that Pinkey is so well — I hope it may long Continue & that She may not bring back her cough by any imprudence. — Accept our best thanks for your continued Kindness to her."

Mrs. Williams wrote yet again to Mrs. Barrett on November 4, 1794, indicating that the final amount due on accounts connected with the frame and packing was £14. One is probably justified in assuming that the painting was completed by that date.

In spite of Mrs. Barrett's great eagerness to have the portrait, it was not sent at once to Jamaica. Apparently (although the exchange of letters gives out at this point) Lawrence, well aware of his success with the painting, asked if he might include it among the group he intended to send to the next exhibition at the Royal Academy in the spring of 1795. The Academy exhibition, it must be remembered, was then the great annual art event, as indeed it had been since its inception a quarter of a century earlier. It was in these exhibitions that the reputations of rising young artists were made and those of the established men constantly tested. Lawrence had won his laurels when elected a full academician early in 1794. But his extreme youth and the tendency of many critics to judge him in relation to his older but less highly lauded colleagues meant that he could never relax in these early years. Small wonder, accordingly, that he would request permission to retain for the exhibition such an unusual and remarkable painting as "Pinkie." From the point of view of the sitter and her family there would also be some satisfaction in seeing the portrait so highly regarded. And so it was that the picture remained in England to make its appearance as Number 75, "Portrait of a Young Lady," in the Royal Academy exhibition that opened at the beginning of May 1795.

But just a week before that date, tragedy struck. Pinkie died on April 23, 1795. She was buried on April 30 at St. Alfege's, Greenwich, on the eve of the opening of the exhibition. We do not know what caused her death, but her grandmother's rather ominous reference to a cough in one of the letters to Mrs. Williams suggests that Pinkie, like so many of her contemporaries, may have been a victim of tuberculosis. It is a sad irony that the first public appearance of the portrait must have taken on (at least in the minds of the sitter's family and the artist) the character of a memorial occasion.

Curiously enough, in view of the great popularity of the painting today, "Pinkie" seems to have passed virtually unnoticed at the exhibition of 1795. In fact Lawrence generally received scant attention from the critics that year. His competitors, Hoppner, Beechey, and Northcote, ran off with most of the acclaim. Hoppner in particular seems to have been the most favored artist of the moment. He was chosen to paint the portrait of the new Princess of Wales, a suggestion defended by *The Times* with the comment: "His merit is so undoubted that his brother artists cannot reasonably complain of the preference given to him."

After the Royal Academy exhibition Pinkie's portrait moved into the private collection of her family and was not again seen publicly for more than one hundred years. One basic detail in the subsequent history of the painting is unfortunately obscure. We do not know whether in fact it ever made the journey across the Atlantic to Jamaica. A letter of October 12, 1795, to Mrs. Williams from her sister in Jamaica states, "poor Pinky's picture has never been heard of — Hibberts says it never was sent to his house he knows nothing of it." But this uncertainty aside, by the middle of the first decade of the nineteenth century the portrait was in London in the possession of Pinkie's brother Edward, the father of the poet Elizabeth Barrett Browning. It remained with members of the Moulton-Barrett family (Pinkie's brother added the "Barrett" to his name in 1798) until the early years of this century. Its second public appearance, one hundred and twelve years after the first, was again at the Royal Academy, in the Old Masters Exhibition of 1907. The success it had there prompted a reappearance at an exhibition a year later at Agnew's. In 1910 the then owner, Mrs. Maria Elizabeth Moulton-Barrett, parted with the painting by private sale to Agnew (the art dealer). It subsequently entered Lord Michelham's collection. When Lord Michelham's pictures were auctioned on November 24, 1926, the portrait was acquired by Duveen for 74,000 guineas, then considered to be the highest price ever paid for a painting at open auction. "Pinkie" passed into the Huntington collection less than two months later in January of 1927. It was Mr. Huntington's last major painting purchase before his death on May 23, 1927.

Ever since the arrival of "Pinkie" in the Huntington collection the painting has been closely linked with "The Blue Boy"; this association is understandable, for the paintings form in many respects a natural pair. And yet the differences are more imposing and fundamental than the similarities. "The Blue Boy" is a magnificent act of homage on Gainsborough's part to the artist he admired above all others, the seventeenth-century portraitist Van Dyck. Gainsborough painted it apparently for his own pleasure, unimpeded by the restrictions that would normally hedge about a regular portrait commission. The measure of Lawrence's achievement in "Pinkie" is found precisely in the converse of this situation. There is nothing in the record to suggest that from his point of view the painting began as anything more than a routine portrait commission, involving a sitter of no particular importance, with whom he had no personal connection. Possibly the most remarkable thing about the painting is that from these distinctly unexceptional circumstances Lawrence should produce such a vital and fresh portrait that has rightly taken its place in the popular estimation as embodying the very spirit of English childhood.

Pinkie is probably the most famous among Lawrence's many highly successful portraits of children. The scintillating brushwork and fresh, brisk color convey something of the sparkle of youth. Like so many of his artistic contemporaries, however, Lawrence could vary his means when a different expression was called for. His range is not so wide as Reynolds', but he is capable of capturing many nuances in the personalities of his sitters. One's admiration for his achievement in "Pinkie" is increased when the painting is seen beside others of different types. The portraits of Warren Hastings (1811) (*Fig. 46*) and Lady Blessington (1822) (*Fig. 47*) are excellent indications of Lawrence's ability to capture totally different characters on canvas. The most interesting point about the comparison of these pictures is that the contrast is created without using the sort of learned machinery and play on associations that Reynolds is likely to have employed. The composition in the portrait of Hastings is of the utmost simplicity, the two light areas of the head and the hands balancing one another to reinforce the air of quiet dignity and restraint, thoroughly appropriate for the portrait of this statesman towards the end of his tragic career. Lady Blessing-

Fig. 47. Sir Thomas Lawrence, *Countess of Blessington*, canvas, 35 x 27¾ ins. (The Wallace Collection, London).

g. *46*. Sir Thomas Lawrence, *Warren Hastings*, nvas, 35½ x 27½ ins. (The National ortrait Gallery, London).

ton is all feminine elegance and grace. Her portrait, in contrast to the organization in terms of light and dark used for Warren Hastings, is essentially an elaborate linear study in compound sinuous curves, moving both over the surface of the painting and into suggested depth. Lawrence's means for achieving the totally different moods of these two portraits involves the most basic language of painting — a change from a tonal, stable, planar organization to one that is linear, in restless motion, and operating spatially as well as on the surface of the picture. And both are quite different from the fresh, sparkling mood of "Pinkie." So Lawrence also exhibits, although in a less blatant way than some of his contemporaries, the typically romantic interest in range and variety of emotional expression which we noted in the first chapter of this book as one of the salient features of the period.

[1] This and other letters relating to the painting were first published by Philip Kelley and Ronald Hudson, "New Light on Sir Thomas Lawrence's 'Pinkie,'" *Huntington Library Quarterly*, XXVIII (1965), 255-61.

Fig. 48. Thomas Rowlandson, *Mrs. Siddons Rehearsing*, pen and watercolor, 12½ x 9 ins.

Chapter VI

Rowlandson's
"Mrs. Siddons Rehearsing"

WITHIN A YEAR OR TWO of the time Reynolds exhibited his great portrait of "Mrs. Siddons as the Tragic Muse," Thomas Rowlandson drew a highly entertaining comic portrait of the same actress. Rowlandson shows Mrs. Siddons rehearsing in the Green Room, being coached by her father Roger Kemble, while another actor declaims in front of a mirror in the background. The drawing is an amusing antidote to the rather rhetorical grandeur of Reynolds' portrait. One particularly enjoys the way old Kemble, prompt-book in hand, seems to enter into his daughter's dramatic frenzy, and to urge her on to even greater heights (or depths) of despair. Apparently this very overt type of emotional display was the normal theatrical idiom of the time, although Rowlandson is not likely to have erred in the direction of understatement.

We are not sure exactly when the drawing was made and this is not a matter of great importance. An old inscription on the back states that the third figure to the left is the actor John Henderson, who died in 1785. A date of 1784 or 5, while not impossible, is somewhat earlier for Rowlandson than the technique of the drawing would imply. When the drawing was exhibited in London in 1950 Mr. Gilbert Davis, who then owned it, suggested that the third actor was a man called Hudson, which would allow a little more leeway in dating. Mrs. George in her catalog of the political and personal satires in the British Museum (7591) assigns the drawing to 1789 with a question mark. A date in the later 1780's seems probable, when Mrs. Siddons was still enjoying the full applause of her early London successes.

The Rowlandson drawing is not great art. It would be pretentious and silly to judge it by the standards one applies to other paintings discussed in this book. The medium in which Rowlandson created his picture is pen and watercolor, and for this reason it is normally classed as a "drawing" rather than a "painting." But it is a complete, self-contained work and a good sample of a large body of drawing that occupies an important place in the Georgian scene. An awareness of this material is essential for any balanced estimate of the art of the period.

Humor is fortunately a widespread human characteristic, and it has taken graphic form in one way or another from remote antiquity to the present day. But there is hardly any other period when comic art reached the level both in quantity and quality that it did in late eighteenth and early nineteenth-century England. The reasons for this phenomenon are impossible to pin down. National temperament may be a factor. Also the romantic state of mind, which was dominant at the time, encompassed humor, caricature and the grotesque within the range of emotional sensations it delighted to explore. But it is more difficult to explain why comic drawing attained such status as art, engaging the talents of a host of gifted draftsmen who produced quantities of drawings that were clearly to be treated as works of art and not merely as humorous ephemera.

Thomas Rowlandson is the most popular of this numerous breed, and that is as it should be. He was incredibly prolific, producing literally thousands of drawings, and was certainly the most genial and versatile of the group. James Gillray may have had a more inventive imagination, but his rather savage brand of humor was concerned primarily with the special area of political caricature. Gillray's drawings, which are comparatively rare, are brilliant and forceful affairs, but were not intended as completed works, as were the highly decorative pen and watercolor creations of Rowlandson. The other men — Bunbury, Woodward, Newton, Isaac Cruikshank, Dighton, Nixon and many more — are altogether of lesser stature, although they all help to swell the great flow of this ingratiating phase of Georgian art.

There are actually several artistic currents that intermingle to produce a drawing such as "Mrs. Siddons Rehearsing," and Rowlandson deserves the primary credit for creating the synthesis that made such a picture possible: a blend of humorous observation with brilliant, virtuoso penwork and highly decorative washes of watercolor. It is a synthesis achieved by Rowlandson in the early 1780's, about half a dozen years before the drawing of Mrs. Siddons, and then retained as the dominant idiom for this type of art in England during half a century.

The national inclination toward humor in art was superbly stated early in the Georgian period by William Hogarth. Hogarth's humor has a strong satiric tinge and ultimately therefore a serious purpose that is not nearly so apparent in his numerous progeny. Most of these, including Rowlandson, are usually content to record what is funny and entertaining in the world around them without drawing a moral. There are very few of the sources of visual humor that Hogarth did not understand and exploit. For him, the end artistic product for his designs was normally an engraving, produced and sold in quantity. In preparation for these prints Hogarth created both paintings and drawings. The paintings, such as the "Marriage à la Mode" series, are among the most brilliant and sparkling productions in the whole range of British art.

They are, of course, vastly more impressive than Rowlandson's watercolors. But whereas Hogarth produced perhaps two dozen of these masterpieces during his lifetime, hundreds of drawings flowed from Rowlandson's facile pen each year for nearly five decades. Hogarth's actual drawings are few in number. Almost invariably they are preparatory studies for his prints; they are usually executed in red or black pencil, and clearly were never intended as self-contained works of art. There is none of the masterful penwork and enlivening watercolor of Rowlandson's drawings, although Hogarth, in a more informal way, frequently reveals an incisive power and bite that is beyond Rowlandson's range. Rowlandson must have known the Hogarth prints intimately. They would have been all around him in every collector's portfolio. Although Hogarth died when Rowlandson was only six, the prints retained great popularity throughout the eighteenth century. It was surely Hogarth, through the medium of his prints, who taught Rowlandson to look about and catch the humor in his immediate environment. But equally surely Hogarth was not the source for Rowlandson's virtuoso penwork and the highly decorative washes with which he enlivens his drawings. In these matters the younger man had other teachers.

The other currents of artistic activity that contributed most to Rowlandson's achievement were the tradition of caricature, particularly portrait caricature, that developed in mid-eighteenth-century Italy, and the narrative wash or watercolor drawing that was produced in mid-eighteenth-century France.

The closely related interests in caricature and the grotesque have a long history in Italy going back at least as far as Leonardo da Vinci. Agostino Carracci, and even Bernini, made contributions to this genre in the seventeenth century. By the early eighteenth century portrait caricature was a well-developed art in Italy, usually taking the form of line drawing. The best-known practitioner was Pier Leone Ghezzi. The young English gentry, who always included a lengthy stay in Italy on their Grand Tour of Europe, seem to have particularly enjoyed caricatures, and brought back a goodly number with them. British artists who travelled to Italy were frequently infected with this craze. One in particular, Thomas Patch (1725-1782), ultimately made a specialty of this art form. He settled in Florence where he drew many of his compatriots as they sojourned in that city. Patch's caricatures exist as paintings, drawings, and prints (*Fig. 49*). The drawings and prints reflect closely the style of men like Ghezzi. The drawings were sometimes undertaken with engraving specifically in mind and most of them use a system of parallel-line shadings and hatchings that could be transferred directly to the print.

Patch does not employ his caricatures in the service of any program of social or political reform. They seem invariably to be simply good-natured spoofs, picking out and exaggerating some characteristic feature of his subject, but with no moralizing or malicious intention. Most of the drawings and prints are of

Fig. 49. Thomas Patch, *Spencer Draper*, etching.

single figures. The paintings usually depict groups, following the general format of the contemporary conversation piece portraits. They were all undertaken at least with the full permission of the people portrayed. It seems likely in fact that most of the pictures were made on commission from those who were the objects of the caricature.

The prints of Ghezzi and Patch must have become widely known in England during the 1750's and 60's, and they add a new dimension to the comic art of the period as it was then developing through the works of Hogarth. It is particularly from the point of view of technique that the Italian drawings are of interest in the British development. The medium in these continental sketches was line, developed and exploited in a way that seldom appears in the graphic works of Hogarth. And line is the basis of Rowlandson's, and indeed of most late eighteenth-century British comic art.

The earliest works by Rowlandson that we know come from the late 1770's and are in a stylistic idiom closely related to that of Ghezzi and Patch. Rowlandson would certainly have seen these popular prints, and he was probably also familiar with the work of other English artists, such as J. H. Mortimer and the amateur, Lord Townshend, who were adopting a similar style at just about the same time. But if a drawing such as "The Dissection" (*Fig. 50*) is technically related to this linear style imported from Italy, other aspects of this sketch already indicate a distinct personality at work. There is a concern with the macabre and grotesque which reminds one much more of Mortimer, or (more remote in time) Hogarth's "Four Stages of Cruelty," than the relatively benign and good-humored productions of Ghezzi and Patch.

The number of drawings by Rowlandson now known that were produced during the 1770's is very small. It seems virtually certain that many more must survive but have been overlooked because they are, superficially at least, so unlike Rowlandson's later work. These drawings are all executed in pen alone, without the enlivening washes of watercolor that are such a handsome decorative addition to Rowlandson's more mature productions. Instead of washes, they employ elaborate systems of parallel lines and hatching to create shadows, a technical detail that emphasizes their affinities with drawings and prints of the type produced by Ghezzi and Patch. The humor, without the mitigating effect of color, seems more harsh and verging on the grotesque than we usually expect from Rowlandson. Already, however, one is aware of a flexibility in the pen work and a virtuoso control that passes noticeably beyond the Continental sources for this style of drawing. Rowlandson's pen line thickens and thins in a way that serves to enhance the three-dimensional character of his figures, and also gives the drawings a calligraphic elegance that is hardly apparent in the work of the earlier men. There is already a tension between an elegant, technical virtuosity and a tendency to vulgar and macabre themes that runs through all of Rowlandson's art, giving it a highly distinctive bittersweet flavor.

Fig. 50. Thomas Rowlandson, *The Dissection*, pen, 14 x 19 ins.

Fig. 51. Paul Sandby, *The Band Box Carrier*, pen and watercolor, 7⅞ x 6¼ ins.

Fig. 52. Louis-Philippe Boitard, *Man Asleep*, pen and watercolor, 6⅞ x 5⅛ ins.

Fig. 53. Charles Brandoin, *The Royal Academy Exhibition, 1771*, watercolor, 9 ⁵/₁₆ x 13³/₄ ins.

One of the many minor mysteries concerning Rowlandson's career is the reason why he gave up this early style of drawing, apparently quite abruptly and definitely in the early 1780's, and adopted the much more lively and decorative use of watercolor washes which he subsequently retained for the rest of his long and productive career. But if we do not know why Rowlandson made this change, there can be little doubt about the pictorial sources that prompted him to move in this direction. These were drawings by French artists, or artists trained in France, that began appearing in increasing numbers in England after the mid-eighteenth century.

The tinted pen drawing was no newcomer to British art at the time it was taken up by Rowlandson. The draftsman Paul Sandby used this technique for some of his figure studies from the 1750's and 60's (*Fig. 51*). But the primary impetus in this direction seems to have come from artists with strong affiliations on the other side of the Channel. One of the earliest of these was a nebulous figure, Louis-Philippe Boitard (apparently the son of the better known François Boitard) who produced (probably about 1750) numerous drawings using a pen and watercolor technique close to that subsequently adopted by Rowlandson thirty years later (*Fig. 52*). But Boitard's drawings are not specifically comic in intention, nor does his penwork have the calligraphic elegance and flexibility characteristic of Rowlandson's work.

Another little-known artist, apparently of French training and active in England during the 1760's, was Charles Brandoin. His drawing of the Royal Academy exhibition for 1771 might at first glance be mistaken for a Rowlandson (*Fig. 53*). The crowd of figures, presented in good humored but mildly satirical fashion, the bustle of a social occasion, the decorative watercolor washes, all anticipate clearly the style Rowlandson would adopt about ten years later. But again there is nothing comparable to Rowlandson's virtuoso penwork.

Yet another artist whose work in the 1770's is like Rowlandson's of a decade later is the Parisian-trained James de Loutherbourg who spent most of his active career in England and explored many art forms. The list could be considerably extended, but enough has been said to indicate that the type of elegant pen and watercolor figure drawing with comic overtones that Rowlandson adopted in the early 1780's was certainly not his invention. Actually one's principal surprise is that he waited as long as he did to use this form, which he must have encountered frequently in London, or at its source in Paris during the mid-1770's. The fact is that we are very ill-informed about the details of Rowlandson's career during the early 1780's. From the art historian's point of view he doesn't come clearly into focus with any documented works until 1784, by which time the transformation from his early monochromatic pen style to his characteristic pen and watercolor drawing was complete. In that year he exhibited at the Academy two of his acknowledged masterpieces, "Vauxhall Gardens" and "Skating on the Serpentine." In the autumn of 1784 he also drew the splendid series of sketches now in the Huntington collection that trace a rather madcap excursion he made with a friend, Henry Wigstead, to the New Forest and Isle of Wight (*Figs. 54 and 55*).

Fig. 54. Thomas Rowlandson, *Tailpiece*, from *Tour in a Post Chaise*, pen and watercolor, 4$\frac{1}{2}$ x 7$\frac{5}{16}$ ins.

Fig. 55. Thomas Rowlandson, *Delay at Popham Lane*, from *Tour in a Post Chaise*, pen and watercolor, 5 x 8 ins.

Rowlandson never produced anything better than these drawings of 1784. They are bubbling over with vitality and good humor, and represent a most attractive fusion of the spirited pen work which the artist had developed during the 1770's and his new-found facility with watercolor. As his career progressed, Rowlandson's use of line loses some of the verve it has in these early works; the penwork becomes tighter and more mechanical, although throughout his life he retains as his basic idiom the combination of pen and watercolor which he evolved in the 1780's.

The drawing of Mrs. Siddons is certainly not far in date from this early peak in Rowlandson's art. The sketch, like so many of his more popular inventions, has lost some of its punch by too much exposure to daylight, so that the washes are somewhat faded. The comparatively large scale of the drawing, and the portrait element involved, mean that the penwork is not so free as in smaller sketches of contemporary date, such as the "Tailpiece" to the 1784 tour. But the mood of the drawing is very much that of Rowlandson of the 1780's. He restrains, for instance, the tendency toward gross caricature in which he frequently indulges later in life, and for which Mrs. Siddon's notoriously long nose must have offered a particularly inviting opportunity. How cruel Rowlandson could become in such matters is well illustrated by his caricatures of the singer Mme. Catalani (*Fig. 56*) and the instrumentalists Johann Christian Bach and Karl Friedrich Abel (*Fig. 57*). One would be hard put to recognize the face of the last from Gainsborough's superb portrait of this rather handsome and benign court musician. Mrs. Siddons is notably spared this sort of treatment and the

Fig. 56. Thomas Rowlandson, *Mme. Catalani,* pen and watercolor, 9 x 7¼ ins.

Fig. 57. Thomas Rowlandson, *Concerto Spirituale,* pen and watercolor, 7¾ x 6½ ins.

Fig. 58. Thomas Rowlandson, *A French Frigate Towing an English Man-O-War into Port*, pen and watercolor, 10½ x 8¼ ins.

drawing is a readily recognizable portrait. Although the sketch is certainly comic, it is hardly a caricature, except possibly in the treatment of Kemble, Mrs. Siddon's father.

It is only fair to Rowlandson, who is often classed simply as a caricaturist, to point out that he had many more strings to his bow; that he is in fact a remarkably versatile artist, and that even his purely comic drawings are seldom dependent entirely on caricature. Caricature, properly defined, is the art of exaggerating for comic and expressive effect some salient physical characteristic of a person. Rowlandson, as the drawing of Mme. Catalani indicates, certainly understood the principles of caricature; but the humor in his drawings is more likely to depend on his grasp of some comic action or situation. This is surely the basis of the humor in the sketch of Mrs. Siddons. A much more subtle type of perception and imagination is involved, and a much richer form of humor results.

Rowlandson also has great skill in complementing and reinforcing the fun in a drawing with an appropriate caption. We are so accustomed to this type of art today in the modern cartoon that we tend to take it for granted; but the idea of a play between words and picture, where both are essential for the full comic effect, is a rather sophisticated conception. Hogarth used the device extensively, and nearly all of his comic prints are supplemented in an important way by the captions that went with them. In the hands of Rowlandson and his contemporaries the idea was sharpened and given much greater punch. The drawing inscribed "A French Frigate towing an English Man-o-War into Port" is highly entertaining in itself (*Fig. 58*). But the caption gives the humor an edge that would otherwise be lost. Both the drawing and the caption are necessary for the full effect; the two are inextricably interwoven.

Rowlandson's perennial popularity from his own day to this is the result of many factors. The most important of these is certainly his sense of humor. This is strongly supported by his astute observation of the social scene about him, making his drawings an inexhaustible compendium of the manners of the time. But from a more purely aesthetic point of view he is a brilliant draftsman; at his best, probably the most accomplished master of line-drawing England has ever produced. Furthermore, his sensitively handled washes of watercolor give his drawings a decorative effect that provides just the right counterbalance to the slightly gross and vulgar themes with which he is usually involved. In his particular combination of talents he is one of the most original and immediately appealing of all English artists.

Fig. 59. William Blake, *Satan, Sin, and Death* (1808), pen and watercolor, 19¹/₂ x 15¹³/₁₆ ins.

Chapter VII

Blake's "Satan, Sin and Death"

WILLIAM BLAKE AND THOMAS ROWLANDSON were close contemporaries. They probably were acquainted, but it seems highly unlikely that they would have had much to say to each other. Two artists more different temperamentally it would be difficult to imagine. There is, however, a close affinity at least in technique: Blake and Rowlandson both worked primarily in the pen and water-color medium. But whereas Rowlandson applied his talent to close observation of the society that surrounded him, Blake's sources are largely literary, supplemented by his own incredibly fertile imagination.

Blake was a poet as well as a draftsman, and his most distinctive achievements, in his illustrated books, involve a fusion of words and pictures that is entirely personal. Any total estimate of Blake as an artist must deal with this composite art-form he developed, the interweaving of the verbal and visual, each supplementing the other to create a whole much greater than the sum of the parts. Let it be said at once that what follows in this chapter concerns only the visual side of Blake's work, so that those to whom such a fragmented estimate is anathema, or whose interest in Blake stems from his poetry, can pass without further delay to another section.

Blake's art is so unlike the portraits and landscapes that dominate Georgian painting that it is frequently regarded as an isolated phenomenon. And indeed, his illuminated books have no real precedent or parallel. But his independent drawings are less unusual. They are simply the highest peak in a long range of artistic activity that stretches from the mid-eighteenth to the mid-nineteenth century. But placing Blake in historical context in no way diminishes his stature. On the contrary, it enables us to see how superior he is to his predecessors and contemporaries who aspired in a similar direction.

"Satan, Sin and Death," also called "Satan comes to the Gates of Hell," is a powerful and characteristic example of Blake's mature work. He is not here creating a design to accompany his own writings but an illustration to Milton's *Paradise Lost*, a poem that was particularly attractive to artists in Blake's day. Illustrations to *Paradise Lost* (and also to the plays of Shakespeare) form an interesting gauge by which to measure the developing romantic spirit in England. The high tide for both is just around the turn of the eighteenth to the nineteenth century. The twenty years from 1790 to 1810 saw the appearance of at least fifteen illustrated editions of *Paradise Lost* as well as Henry Fuseli's highly ambitious "Milton Gallery." The last was no doubt inspired by John Boydell's slightly earlier Shakespeare Gallery, a grandiose scheme to which many of the leading English painters of the day contributed. Blake never became deeply engrossed with Shakespearian subjects, but he certainly shared the widespread enthusiasm for Milton. During the first decade of the nineteenth century he created sets of illustrations not only to *Paradise Lost*, but also *Comus* and "On the Morning of Christ's Nativity." Drawings for all these projects (none of which appeared in printed form at the time) are in the Huntington collection.

The episode illustrated in "Satan, Sin and Death" comes from *Paradise Lost*, Book II lines 645 ff. Satan, on his way to undertake the temptation of Adam and Eve, is stopped by Death at the gate of Hell. They engage in combat but are separated by Sin, "woman to the waste, and fair, but ended foul in many a scaly fauld," who discloses that Death is in fact the son of Sin and Satan. This particular episode caught the attention of artists. It is included in the very first illustrated edition of *Paradise Lost* in 1688 and it appears again and again throughout the eighteenth century. Blake himself treated the theme twice, with minor variations, in 1807 and 1808, and both of his versions happen to be in the Huntington collection (*Figs. 59 and 60*).

Blake's design is an impressive achievement that manages to convey something of the awesome grandeur and superhuman forces involved in this confrontation. There are many things that account for the success of the picture. The heroic proportions of the figures, and the idea of making Death into a transparent wraith immediately transport the event beyond the physical world. But probably the most important factor in determining our reaction is the strong abstract organization imposed upon the arrangement. The complementary positions of Satan and Death, with Sin between, are so contrived that the contours of the limbs and the spears of the two protagonists create a system of diagonal accents that greatly reinforces the sense of opposition between the two male figures and also the efforts of Sin to keep them apart. Furthermore these diagonal accents are made even more eloquent by being played against a grid of verticals and horizontals in the background.

This strong interest in rhythmic and expressive linear pattern is at the very core of Blake's art. To achieve it he does not hesitate to modify details of anatomy or pose so that the linear accents created by the contours will move with a minimum of interruption. Also, in order to give this pattern maximum play, he normally arranges his figures in a shallow frieze-like space that encourages the spectator to concentrate on the outlines rather than explore any effects of depth and recession. The uncompromising concern with pattern and abstract

Fig. 60. William Blake, *Satan, Sin, and Death* (1807), pen and watercolor,
9³/₄ x 8³/₁₆ ins.

Fig. 61. William Hogarth, *Satan, Sin, and Death*, canvas, 24⅜ x 29⅜ ins.
(The Tate Gallery, London).

organization also tends to remove Blake's figures from the normal range of human experience, which makes us more willing to accept the visionary events and creatures with which he deals.

Blake brought this type of linear expression to a level unsurpassed by any other English artist, but he is certainly not alone in developing the technique. The trend toward this form of organization can be followed through earlier illustrations to the same episode in *Paradise Lost*. Hogarth tried his hand at the subject, and his version was later engraved by Rowlandson. Henry Fuseli illustrated the scene more than once. James Barry included it among his illustrations to *Paradise Lost* made in the 1790's, and James Gillray thought the subject sufficiently familiar to use it as the basis of a particularly vicious political cartoon in 1792. These are only a few of the better-known representations of the subject.[1] Blake had probably seen many of these designs, and some recollection of them had likely been stored away in his capacious visual memory, but he outdistances them all in expressive intensity.

The Hogarth treatment is not a very awesome affair (*Fig. 61*). The essentially rococo idiom within which he works, and which he never fully succeeds in escaping, cannot be successfully adapted to powerful emotional expression. The composition lacks controlling dynamic accents; there is little sense of conflict. The figures grimace and strike poses, but the imagination of the spectator is not deeply stirred. This, like the climax scene of "Marriage à la Mode," is one of those instances when Hogarth's intention to be forceful is evident, and one commends the effort without being much impressed by the result.

Henry Fuseli's painting is more successful (*Fig. 62*). Fuseli, a Swiss artist who lived in England during most of his career, became a friend of Blake later in the century. They knew and admired each other's work, and there was some borrowing of motifs back and forth. Fuseli referred to Blake's designs as "damned good to steal from." Blake in turn regarded Fuseli as "The only man that e'er I knew Who did not make me almost spew." Blake was still in his teens when Fuseli (then in Italy) made his first drawing of "Satan, Sin and Death." But Fuseli returned to the subject on at least two other occasions during his career, so Blake would have had ample opportunity to study his friend's treatment of the theme. The heroic, idealized forms contribute to the stronger emotional impact of the Fuseli painting in relation to the Hogarth design. The figures are supported by the dynamic composition created by the arms and legs. The contours or outlines of the bodies are emphasized in a way that creates a much more emphatic abstract organization than is present in the Hogarth design and this organization adds to the idea of opposition and conflict.

These qualities are developed even further and more effectively in James Barry's engraving of the subject (*Fig. 63*). Barry, like Fuseli, was about fifteen years older than Blake. Although there is no evidence that Blake and Barry ever were close friends, they probably met. Certainly Blake expressed his admiration for the older man on many occasions, and even projected a poem entitled

Fig. 62. Henry Fuseli, *Satan, Sin, and Death,* canvas, 26½ x 23 ins. (Los Angeles County Museum of Art).

Fig. 63. James Barry, *Satan, Sin, and Death,* engraving.

"Barry." Barry, like Blake subsequently, compresses his figures into a comparatively shallow space in order to give maximum effect to the strong pattern of opposed diagonal accents. And he further heightens the feeling of tension by modeling the figures with exaggerated light and shadow, accentuating the way their bulk fills and even overflows the limited space.

Barry had developed this expressive linear idiom at least twenty years before he employed it in the "Satan, Sin and Death" design, and it is through him more than any other artist that it became established as an important current in late eighteenth-century British art. Barry was born in 1741 in Cork where he passed his youth and learned, probably through studying prints, some rudiments of art. In the 1760's he came to the attention of his great compatriot Edmund Burke, who brought him to London, introduced him to men like Reynolds, and subsequently supported him for a prolonged period of study in Italy. It was during these years in the late 1760's, mostly in Rome, that his style was formed. He returned to England in 1771, was elected an associate of the newly founded Royal Academy in 1772, and a full academician in the following year. He was appointed Professor of Painting at the Academy in 1782. During the last thirty years of the eighteenth century Barry was greatly admired and respected, especially by younger artists such as Blake.

The style that Barry brought back with him from Italy is epitomized by his small painting, "Mercury Inventing the Lyre," exhibited at the Royal Academy in 1774. (*Fig. 64*). What catches the eye immediately is the flowing, attenuated contour of the figure. Line, as created by contour, is clearly Barry's primary concern and it remains so throughout his career. The tendency to compose in terms of rhythmic contours is even more explicit in some of Barry's early drawings, where (like Blake a couple of decades later) he does not hesitate to modify anatomy if the flow and pattern is sustained in this way (*Fig. 65*).

But early in his career Barry developed an ability to manipulate and control these linear patterns for a variety of expressive effects, and this is something he also passed on to other artists such as Blake. The "Satan, Sin and Death" has a totally different expressive impact from "Mercury Inventing the Lyre." The clashing diagonal accents establish a completely different mood from the gentle undulating lines in the earlier picture. Although these pictures are about twenty years apart, Barry is capable of making this sort of adjustment at any point in his career. This acceptance of, and indeed desire for, a wide range of emotional expression is characteristic of much late eighteenth-century art. The vacillation, as it appears in Barry's work, is of particular interest because there are some specific connections with the theoretical speculation on such matters. In the late 1750's Barry's friend and patron Edmund Burke produced a very influential book, *A Philosophical Enquiry into the Origin of our Ideas of the Sublime and Beautiful*. Burke recognized that we respond aesthetically to various types of objects and sensations. He divided these into two general categories. One,

Fig. 64. James Barry, *Mercury Inventing the Lyre*, canvas, 27½ x 29½ ins.
(Lord Egremont).

Fig. 65. James Barry, *St. Sebastian*, pen
and wash, 10¾ x 6¾ ins. (The National
Gallery of Ireland).

which he called the beautiful, had to do with pleasurable sensations and was produced by objects that were small, with gently undulating, flowing contours, smooth, clear, light and delicate. The other sensation, which Burke called the sublime, was related to the awesome and terrifying. It was created by objects that were vast, rugged, straight or with marked deviations, dark and gloomy, massive.

Burke's elaboration of these two divergent realms of sensation is symptomatic of the growing interest of the late eighteenth century in exploring a wider range of expression than had normally been considered acceptable in art. Although there were many earlier artists who were exponents of either the beautiful or sublime as Burke understood the terms, there were very few that assumed both as their province and ranged freely from one to the other. Clearly Barry did, and regardless of the success we may feel he achieved, the attempt to control these two areas of expression is obvious enough. It would seem also that Barry was directly influenced by Burke in the physical qualities that he associates with the beautiful and sublime. The differences between "Mercury Inventing the Lyre" and "Satan, Sin and Death" reflect the ideas of Burke in the apparent relative size of the objects, the character of the contours and linear accents, the use of light and shadow. Barry's willingness and ability to make these adjustments in his manner of drawing in order to create differences in mood is an interesting instance of the growing consciousness within the late eighteenth century of form as something that can be manipulated, a situation which (as pointed out in Chapter I) had its most extreme statement in the architecture of the period.

Blake certainly shared with Barry an ability to adjust his compositions for a variety of expressive effects. The "Creation of Eve" (*Fig. 66*), also from the *Paradise Lost* series, is an eloquent comparison with "Satan, Sin and Death" from this point of view. The basic organization in terms of verticals and horizontals, the smaller scale of the figures relative to the picture area, create an expression of quiet stability and comparative spaciousness that is in marked contrast to the turbulence, and sense of opposition and compression in "Satan, Sin and Death." But if Barry and Blake had similar ideas about the sublime and the beautiful, their drawings are easily distinguishable in other ways.

The one British artist whose work comes seriously close to Blake's, and then only at times, is his good friend the sculptor John Flaxman. The relative reputations of Blake and Flaxman are an interesting indication of the shifting tides of taste. In the early nineteenth century, when Blake was known to only a few initiates, Flaxman enjoyed international fame. He was probably the most esteemed English artist of his day, and he was tremendously influential, especially through his engraved illustrations to classical authors. Flaxman's reputation slipped slowly but steadily downhill during the late nineteenth and early twentieth centuries, even as Blake's gradually ascended. It is only in the last

Fig. 66. William Blake, *Creation of Eve*, pen and watercolor, 10 x 8³/₁₆ ins.

decade or so that there has been any serious revival of interest in Flaxman's work, and at present he is still a long way from offering any opposition to Blake at the popularity polls. From a simple visual point of view it is a situation not easy to explain convincingly. Flaxman doesn't have the literary component to his personality that contributes strongly to the fascination Blake exercises. Flaxman's drawings lack something of the rhythmic flow and elegance of Blake's best designs; his line is tighter and harder, and he never enriches his drawings with the watercolors that Blake uses so effectively. But as an illustrator Flaxman's invention and imagination are quite as rich as Blake's, and he has fewer of the weaknesses in drawing that often interfere with the enjoyment of Blake's work. A couple of comparable designs by both artists indicate more quickly and effectively than any verbal description how close the two men can be (*Figs. 67 and 68*).

The relations between Blake and Flaxman, especially in the early parts of their careers, have never been clearly worked out, and it is doubtful if the documents exist that would provide any detailed information on this score. Flaxman's

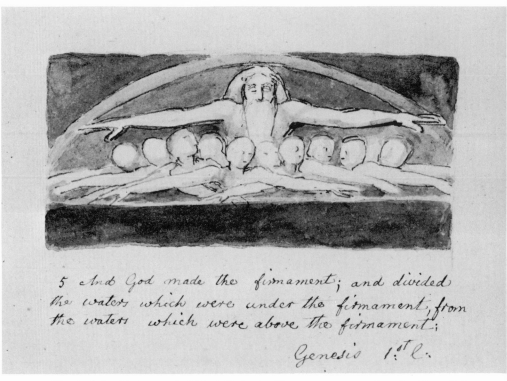

Fig. 67. John Flaxman, *And God Made the Firmament*, pen and wash, 4⅛ x 5⅝ ins.

Fig. 68. William Blake, *David Delivered Out of Many Waters*, pen and watercolor, 16⅜ x 13⅝ ins. (The Tate Gallery, London).

early drawings, from the 1770's, suggest contact with men such as J. H. Mortimer and James Barry, but by the 1780's he had developed the much sparer linear style which, with some refinements, remains his characteristic idiom throughout his life. It is also during these years that Blake evolves from his relatively conventional drawings of the 1770's to the idiom that becomes the basis of his mature art. The two men must have seen a good deal of each other's work at this time, and through the rest of their careers. The question who most influenced whom is academic, and cannot be answered. There can be no doubt, however, about the strong bond that exists between the two men.

But if Blake's basic stylistic vocabulary has affiliations with that of artists such as Fuseli, Barry, and Flaxman, the total expression of his art is some distance removed from that of these men, and certainly is not fully explainable in terms of these connections. Barry, beside Blake, looks mundane, Fuseli looks theatric, Flaxman looks stiff. There is about Blake's work a quality one rather lamely calls "visionary" that places his drawings apart from those of his contemporaries.

The particular qualities of Blake's art are, of course, an outgrowth of his personality, and are connected with his poetic sensibilities, which far outdistance those of the other members of his circle. Another factor of importance is Blake's conviction concerning the relation of his art to the physical world about him. In this matter he takes a more extreme position than most of his friends, and one that would be regarded as radical by the other artists considered in this volume. These men never seriously questioned the premise that their art was founded on a study of "nature." They had, of course, differing notions about what constituted nature. Hogarth and Rowlandson gave their attention to minute particulars, recording everything that is singular in a face or figure. Constable adopted a closely related attitude toward landscape, creating what are in essence portraits of particular places. Reynolds had a more sophisticated relation to the physical world. He felt that the artist could, when occasion required, respond directly to what he saw, as did Hogarth, Rowlandson and Constable. But in accordance with his ideas about the moral and ethical purpose of art, he believed that a nobler form of expression resulted when the artist abstracted an "ideal nature" from the world about him — eliminating what was accidental (and hence imperfect) in an individual figure, and penetrating to the general form common to all objects of the same type but not fully present in any one. Wilson had a comparable attitude toward landscape. Blake, as far as one can judge from his art itself and the rather cryptic statements he makes about it, rejected these various ideas. The artist's source of inspiration was his imagination, a vision from on high, rather than anything based on or distilled from observation of the world about him. Of course, as far as his art is concerned, Blake's imagination was ultimately controlled by the visual images he had stored there, based on what he had observed in the physical world and the creations of other artists. Consequently what emerges is full of reminiscences, most of them probably quite unconscious, of various things seen, including other works of art. The important factor, however, is Blake's sense of emancipation from the physical world as the source of his art. He feels it totally unnecessary to make his figures conform to any norm or ideal other than his own vision of what they should be. Thus, the critic, steeped in more traditional forms and values, who points to the many apparent anomalies in Blake's draftsmanship, to his eccentric and inaccurate presentation of anatomy, to his quite arbitrary canons of proportion, to his apparent inability to handle effectively problems of modeling and fore-shortening, should realize that these details are no part of Blake's concern; that the fertility of his imagination and the strength of his designs are the important considerations. Certainly this is true, and in the best of Blake's drawings the spectator is swept past such shortcomings by the power and originality of his ideas. Nor should one ever forget that the visual is only one component of Blake's art. "Satan, Sin and Death" is much closer to being a literal illustration to an existing text than is usually the case with Blake's designs. More often, and particularly in his illuminated books, the visual side of Blake's work must be studied in close conjunction with the verbal, the one complementing and elucidating the other. It is in this virtually unique composite art form he developed rather than in independent drawings such as "Satan, Sin and Death" that Blake's reputation is highest and most secure.

[1] For further illustrations of this episode see Marcia R. Pointon, *Milton and English Art* (Manchester, 1970).

Fig. 69. Richard Wilson, *River Scene with Bathers*, canvas, 35⅛ x 56⅛ ins.

Chapter VIII

Wilson's "River Scene with Bathers"

PROBABLY THE MOST LASTING IMPRESSION made on many people by Richard Wilson's "River Scene with Bathers" is of the golden light that suffuses the painting. It is the sort of light we associate with a warm summer evening. Actual sunlight doesn't often have such a mellow tone, but this color accords perfectly with the image many of us hold of what evening light ideally should be. Almost everything about the painting has a similar elysian quality. None of us has ever seen a view exactly like this one, and yet (for most people) it immediately strikes a sympathetic chord: the cattle lazing in the late sun while the herders take a swim; the softly rounded hills with masses of unruffled foliage; the quiet river meandering toward the distant mountain and the still more distant, unclouded horizon. There is even a ruined temple, picturesquely placed on a promontory, as a gentle reminder of the transitory character of man's achievement in the face of nature. Everything about the painting contributes to this idyllic mood. It is all a little too good to be true; but we wish it might be true.

Richard Wilson himself had never seen this view, any more than we have, because it doesn't exist. It was for him, as it is for us, an ideal landscape, sensitively developed in his imagination from his recollections of things encountered, both in nature and in art. To the mid-twentieth century, conditioned by the nineteenth-century idea of landscape painting as concerned with capturing some quality associated with a particular view, this notion of landscape as a product of the imagination may seem strange. But it was an attitude that was widely accepted in Wilson's day. The artistic climate that produced a painting such as "River Scene with Bathers" is akin to that which accounts for "Mrs. Siddons as the Tragic Muse." Wilson and Reynolds both had lofty aims for these works of art, and both had clearly developed ideas about how these aims should be achieved.

Underlying the interest in creating an "ideal" landscape was the assumption that art should aspire to something more than mere sensuous gratification; that it should elevate the thoughts of the spectator and purge his mind of petty considerations. This was to be achieved both by *what* was included, and (equally important) the *way* in which it was represented. The scene, with its ruin, spacious vista, and warm summer light, is meant to remind us of Italy, or at least the Mediterranean area, and to arouse by association a train of thought concerned with pastoral idyls of the classical past. But this effect is strongly supported by the way in which Wilson has organized the elements in his painting to sustain a mood of quiet and repose. The picture is carefully balanced around the centrally placed ruin. The hill to the right finds just the proper counterpoise in the distant mountain and the broad stretch of valley to the left. The group of bathers on the left is balanced by the cattle on the right. The whole view is enframed by trees on either side and set comfortably back in space by a dark foreground ledge. The sense of balance, although palpable, is not rigid, and involves many factors, including shape, light, texture and distance. Nothing appears forced, but every element in the picture has been conceived and placed with regard to its relation to the whole.

Wilson spent several years during the early 1750's in Italy where he studied at first hand the type of landscape he wishes to suggest in the Huntington painting. He also at that time came in contact with the work of other artists who had earlier depicted the Italian countryside in idealized views, particularly the paintings of Claude Lorrain, the seventeenth-century French expatriate who spent most of his career in Italy. "River Scene with Bathers" is essentially a subtle synthesis derived from these experiences, woven together in a way that reflects Wilson's own personality and the outlook of his time.

During the years he was in Italy Wilson was particularly active as a draftsman, producing numerous drawings of the buildings and countryside near Rome. The pencil and chalk study of Monte Cavo is an excellent example of these sketches, this one from a large group made on commission for the Earl of Dartmouth (*Fig. 70*). Wilson inscribed the drawings himself with the name of the spot each represents, and there is no doubt he intended them as accurate views of the places depicted. But it is also evident that in making the drawings his eyes tended (probably quite unconsciously) to compose what he saw in terms of the pictorial formulas developed by Claude. The enframing trees, the centrally placed glow on the distant horizon, belong to a type of landscape composition that was perfected by Claude, but which became so popular and widespread in years following that any artist seeking to suggest a mood of lyrical calm in a view would almost automatically adopt this type of organization.

Occasionally, when a particular building rather than a view was the subject of a drawing, this pictorial machinery might be set aside. An interesting instance in connection with the Huntington picture is the sketch of the Temple of Minerva Medica, also from the group executed for the Earl of Dartmouth (*Fig. 71*). Here it was the specific form and construction of the ruined building that caught Wilson's eye and to which he gave his primary attention in the drawing. It is this same ruin that Wilson has incorporated in the Huntington landscape. The fact that he was willing to transpose it to a completely different physical

Fig. 70. Richard Wilson, *Monte Cavo*, black and white chalk, 11½ x 16⅜ ins.

Fig. 71. Richard Wilson, *Temple of Minerva Medica*, black and white chalk, 11¼ x 16½ ins. (Mr. and Mrs. Paul Mellon).

environment from the one in which it actually exists eloquently confirms that the view in the painting is an imaginary one, but compounded from the artist's recollections.

The picture, however, is not only once, but twice removed from reality. At the time Wilson painted the Huntington landscape he was no longer in Italy in direct contact with the motifs from which the picture is composed, but back in England. We cannot say with any precision when "River Scene with Bathers" was painted, but those students who have given most study to Wilson's work think that it probably dates from the early 1770's, some fifteen years after the artist's return from Italy. Insofar as the picture is an imaginary view, the question of where the artist actually was when he painted it may seem of little importance. And yet there is surely a significant difference in attitude and artistic intention between the creation of such a landscape in Italy (where the artist is evolving his ideal from what he sees around him) and in England (many miles and many years away from the elements out of which the scene is developed). In one instance the painting is an idealized view of what the artist has seen in nature; in the other it is a reminiscence of something long since past. This interest in the remote and exotic is characteristic of the age in which Wilson lived, and is one of the preoccupations we associate with the romantic temperament.

There are other features of the painting that also belong to Wilson and his period, and among the most important of these are the way the paint is applied to the canvas and how the particular objects are suggested. For all the reminiscences of Claude in the composition and general mood of the picture, this could never be mistaken for a painting by the seventeenth-century master. It is particularly in the treatment of the foreground elements and the trees to the right that Wilson reveals he is an artist of the mid-eighteenth century. The crisp little daubs of paint with which highlights in the foliage are suggested, as well as the highlights along the edges of the branches and around the rocks, are typical of the decorative handling of pigment in the mid-eighteenth century throughout much of Europe. Wilson, like most of his contemporaries, is more interested in the patterns and shapes created by the trees, foliage, and rocks than he is in suggesting their mass and three-dimensional character. His use of highlights and his concern with silhouette make the trees and rocks on the right foreground into a very eye-catching area of the picture, but one which we respond to primarily as two-dimensional pattern rather than three-dimensional masses. Even in the treatment of the stump in the left foreground, the paint is dabbed on with much more concern for creating a lively area of pigment than suggesting the solidity of the object. In all these respects the way Wilson applies his paint is related to the rococo style, and is unlike the technique of a seventeenth-century artist such as Claude, who was more concerned with effects of mass and depth. It is in the handling of light in the middle ground and atmospheric perspective in the background that Wilson comes closest to seventeenth-century practices.

But even here his paint goes on more thickly and briskly than in the works of Claude.

Wilson thought sufficiently highly of the Huntington composition to repeat it more than once, although always with minor variations (*Figs. 72 and 73*). It is difficult to know how these versions relate to one another in date, as there is

Fig. 72. Richard Wilson, *Landscape with Bathers*, canvas, 23 x 29½ ins. (The Tate Gallery, London).

Fig. 73. Richard Wilson, *Landscape with Bathers*, canvas, 25 x 46 ins. (Leeds City Art Galleries).

nothing but internal evidence to go on. The Huntington picture is physically the largest; it has also been worked out in detail much more fully than the others. The treatment of the ruin is an interesting feature that varies from version to version and may be a helpful clue in dealing with the pictures. The ruin, as it appears in the Huntington landscape, is undoubtedly closely adapted from Wilson's own drawing of the Temple of Minerva Medica. The ruins in the other paintings are similar in general shape, but by no means so close to the actual building that served as the point of departure. It is relatively easy to suppose that the artist in making other paintings derived from the Huntington picture might generalize and change the form of the building somewhat. It is more difficult to imagine him starting with these more generalized buildings and ending up with a depiction that indicates he had gone back to his original drawing; although this possibility cannot be denied. The matter of the ruin would suggest that the Huntington version may be the earliest, and the others are free variants derived from it, rather than that the others are preliminary thoughts later worked up into the more elaborate and finished presentation.

It is an interesting indication of Wilson's pictorial methods that essentially this same composition reappears several times in his work but with different details and an ostensibly different subject. One of these is called "Dolbadarn Castle and Llyn Peris," of which a version is in the National Gallery of Victoria, Melbourne (*Fig. 74*). Here the subject is from Wilson's native Wales, but the organization and composition of the picture are for practical purposes the same as in the Huntington "River Scene with Bathers." Clearly this was a type of composition that Wilson found a satisfactory vehicle for a quiet, idyllic mood. And, as topographical accuracy was not important to his general philosophy of landscape, he felt quite at liberty to reuse this or similar compositions when he was aiming for the mood they evoked. Thus for Wilson the composition or arrangement of the elements was something that could be readily imposed on any motif.

Fig. 74. Richard Wilson, *Dolbadarn Castle and Llyn Peris*, canvas, 37 x 50 ins. (The National Gallery of Victoria, Melbourne).

Wilson had, of course, a large repertory of compositions on which he could call. As far as expression is concerned most of them are related to the gentle, quiet and idyllic. But there were occasions, especially in the earlier part of his career, when he wanted a more turbulent mood, suggesting terror and excitement, akin to what his contemporaries referred to as "the sublime." The best known of Wilson's pictures in this manner is "The Destruction of the Children of Niobe" (*Fig. 75*), which exists in a particularly large number of versions, painted during the 1750's and 60's. In aiming for an effect of turbulence Wilson adopted a different type of composition and a radically different type of light. The stability and calm characteristic of so many of his views is replaced by broken, irregular forms and abrupt contrasts of light and shadow. Once again, in achieving these effects Wilson has had his eye on the work of earlier landscapists, particularly Salvator Rosa, who had developed this type of pictorial organization in the seventeenth century.

What is most interesting about this situation is Wilson's desire to convey such different types of expression in his painting, and his understanding of the fact that to do so he must be prepared to make radical adjustments in the style he employs. Wilson is one of the earliest English painters to exhibit this desire for controlling a wide range of emotion, an outlook that is characteristic of much late eighteenth-century British art, reaching a climax at the end of the century and the beginning of the nineteenth in the work of such architects as Wyatt and Nash, and (where landscape is concerned) the early work of Turner. For Wilson this flexibility is obtained to a great extent in terms of pictorial formulae derived from earlier artists, a procedure that reminds one of the various "revival" and exotic styles that began to make an appearance in architecture at about the same time. But Wilson gives vitality to these formulae by modifying them with his own direct observation of nature and by building his paint surface with a type of brushwork that belongs to him and his contemporaries and is not borrowed from an earlier period.

Fig. 75. Richard Wilson, *Niobe*, canvas, 46 x 66 ins.
(destroyed during World War II, photo courtesy
The Tate Gallery, London).

Fig. 76. Thomas Gainsborough, *The Cottage Door*, canvas, 58 x 47 ins.

Chapter IX

Gainsborough's "The Cottage Door"

DURING HIS LIFETIME Gainsborough's great reputation rested primarily on his work as a portraitist, and this has since continued to be the case. But his first love was for landscape painting, and his initial attraction was to the countryside that surrounded him. A close friend, writing of Gainsborough shortly after his death, said "Nature was his teacher and the woods of Suffolk his academy; here he would pass in solitude his mornings, in making a sketch of an antiquated tree, a marshy brook, a few cattle, a shepherd and his flock, or any other accidental objects that were presented."[1] Gainsborough retained this intense devotion to landscape and the rural scene throughout his life. But as the development of his career as a portraitist kept him more and more within the confines of urban society, particularly London, his attitude toward the countryside was gradually transformed to take on a quality of nostalgic reminiscence that is different from the direct, immediate experience of nature in his boyhood.

"The Cottage Door," a painting from Gainsborough's later years, is in fact every bit as much a product of the artist's imagination as is Wilson's "River Scene with Bathers." But the character of the imagination and the intentions of the two artists are different. The theme of a peasant family standing by the door of a country cottage is one that haunted Gainsborough during the last decade of his career. He returned to it again and again, working out a beautiful series of variations on the motif, each with a special quality of its own, although all sharing the same general attitude. Why this specific subject had such an attraction for the artist is impossible to say, although it is in complete harmony with the early romantic feelings about rural life that were widespread in Europe during Gainsborough's lifetime. It is a point of view that finds some of its most articulate presentations in the writings of J. J. Rousseau or Goldsmith's *Deserted Village* and which is also behind such a curious development as Marie Antoinette's "Hameau" at Versailles, where the queen and her ladies-in-waiting used to play at being milkmaids.

Gainsborough's various cottage door paintings have certain features in common. There is usually a mother holding a baby; sometimes there is a man either seated with the rest of the group, or carrying a bundle of faggots toward the cottage. The scene is always set on the steps of a small thatched house, which

Fig. 77. Thomas Gainsborough,
The Cottage Door, (detail).

is almost submerged in a group of trees. The Huntington picture is one of the most successful of the variations on this motif, and its qualities are enhanced by the fine physical condition of the paint. The group of figures consists of five children and a mother holding a baby (*Fig.* 77). The children, their clothes more off than on, are mostly involved in eating. The oldest child, kneeling with his back to us, is helping one of the younger ones (without too much success) cope with some soup-like food while another child holds up a bowl for more. They are ragged children, but plump, rosy and healthy looking. The mother, a handsome young woman, is also very casually dressed; but her hair is arranged in the pompadour style that was fashionable with society ladies in the 1770's. The whole group is a charming blend of fact and fantasy: the children, in their combination of rags and blooming good health; the mother, ostensibly a peasant, but looking more like one of Marie Antoinette's attendants playing at living in the country. The rest of the picture has the same sort of combination of the real and imaginary. The cottage itself, nestling cosily under the trees, is a most improbable structure on close examination. It dissolves into enveloping shadows that reveal only the door, and bits of attractively textured wall and roof. The nearly-dead tree that moves diagonally up from the lower right is covered with a rich assortment of knobby projections that catch the light (from some unknown source) and create wonderful passages of color and paint. The trees billow up in soft, full branches of foliage. The evening light is cool, and the shadows are deep, but the warm tones in the figures and the cottage wall balance these in a way that creates an overall impression of relaxation.

Much of the appeal of the picture comes from the things represented and the train of associations they arouse, but there is also great attraction for the eye in the way Gainsborough has handled and applied his pigment. He creates rich passages of paint, in areas such as the tree trunk and the foliage, that have been brushed on with ease and freedom. The brush strokes themselves, often in undulating, ribbon-like bands, form patterns for the eye to follow, rhythmic sequences that are of the greatest importance in sustaining the lyrical mood that pervades the whole picture. Furthermore, these independent but rhythmical strokes, often of different colors, create areas of paint texture that are in themselves visually appealing. We, in the mid-twentieth century, are particularly attracted by this free, virtuoso handling that demonstrates the artist's control over his medium and the ease with which he suggests the elements that make up the picture. For sheer wizardry in the manipulation of a brush on canvas, Gainsborough is probably the most accomplished of all British painters. And this quality in his work gives it a strong appeal above and beyond the interest we may (or may not) have in the subjects he treats.

The free, rhythmic flow of the brush in a painting such as "The Cottage Door" is closely connected with the procedure we know Gainsborough adopted in creating such pictures. Although there is much in the painting that indicates the artist had observed closely, at one time or another, children, trees, and effects of light, it is most unlikely that he was actually looking at any of these things when he started composing "The Cottage Door." His hand was unimpeded by the necessity for following the form of any specific objects that he had before his eye; the rhythmic flow is the creation of Gainsborough's own visual imagination rather than any actual trees and foliage. We know, however, that he stimulated his imagination in an interesting and unusual way. There are at least three accounts concerning his method. Reynolds wrote in one of his Discourses that Gainsborough constructed "a kind of model of landskips, on his table: composed of broken stones, dried herbs, and pieces of looking-glass, which he magnified and improved into rocks, trees, and water."[2] Another writer gives a somewhat more extended but essentially similar account: "I . . . have more than once set by him of an evening and seen him make models, or rather thoughts, for landscape scenery, on a little, old-fashioned folding oak table, which stood under his kitchen dresser . . . . This table, held sacred for the purpose, he would order to be brought to his parlor, and thereon compose his designs. He would place cork or coal for his foregrounds, make middle grounds of sand and clay, bushes of mosses and lichens, and set up distant woods of broccoli."[3] He also modeled animals and figures to place in these little tableaux, and then illuminated the whole with candles. But clearly (as Reynolds indicates) these miniature landscapes were simply a point of departure, a stimulus to Gainsborough's eye which then transformed them into the flowing hills, trees, and shrubbery that appear in a landscape such as "The Cottage Door." The references made by Reynolds and others to Gainsborough's use of candles in illuminating these tableaux are of particular interest, and are of considerable help in explaining the glowing but arbitrary lighting from several sources that is found in many of his landscapes, and is particularly apparent in "The Cottage Door," where the principal group of figures (according to conditions of depicted natural light) should be in deep shadow.

The evidence concerning the date of "The Cottage Door" is not so precise as one would wish it to be. It is certainly a mature work, but Gainsborough's landscape style, once established, does not evolve in a sufficiently clear-cut way to permit close dating on a "stylistic" basis alone. We know, however, that Gainsborough exhibited a painting on this theme at the Royal Academy in 1780. An anonymous review of the exhibition comments: "The Artist seems to have neglected his Landscape to display the whole force of his genius in a beautiful groupe of children and their mother."[4] The various other versions of the theme that might date from about 1780 all contain more than one adult, including a man carrying faggots. This is not, to be sure, absolutely conclusive evidence, but it gives strong support to a date of 1780 or shortly before for the painting.

Fig. 78. Thomas Gainsborough, *The Cottage Door*, canvas, 47 x 58 ins. (Cincinnati Art Museum).

Fig. 79. Thomas Gainsborough, *The Woodcutter's Return*, canvas, 58½ x 47½ ins. (Lady Oakes).

From a visual point of view the most distinctive quality of the Huntington "Cottage Door" is the clarity and monumentality of the composition. The other versions of the theme have great charms of their own, but they are much more loosely organized, the figures are more freely grouped, and the relation between the figures and the landscape is more casual. In the Cincinnati version (*Fig. 78*) of the subject, for instance, the figures form a rippling cascade across the picture, a type of grouping the artist used in a less attenuated form in a picture belonging to Lady Oakes, probably the earliest in date of Gainsborough's treatments of the theme (*Fig. 79*). The grouping of the figures is even more open in Mrs. Scudamore's "Cottage Door" painted in 1786 (*Fig. 80*). The most interesting of the variations on the theme for comparison with the Huntington version is certainly the "Cottage Door with Peasant Smoking," painted in 1788 at the very end of his career (*Fig. 81*). Superficially the arrangement is very close to the Huntington picture: the figure group and the cottage are in the

Fig. 80. Thomas Gainsborough, *The Cottage Door*, canvas, 38¾ x 48¾ ins. (Mrs. Scudamore).

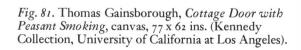

Fig. 81. Thomas Gainsborough, *Cottage Door with Peasant Smoking*, canvas, 77 x 62 ins. (Kennedy Collection, University of California at Los Angeles).

same relative positions, and there is in both a gnarled trunk slanting upwards from the lower right to the center. But the differences within this basically similar format are fascinating. Particularly noticeable are the strong diagonal accents and pyramidal organization in the Huntington picture. The group of figures is firmly knit together within a triangle that is paralleled and re-enforced by the diagonal tree trunk meeting the diagonal path of light up the sky above the head of the young woman. These basic directional accents find many sympathetic echoes. Both triangles are organized along yet another diagonal that moves back into the suggested depth of the landscape from the group of figures to the left background over the little bridge and following the clearing through the forest. The organization of the later painting is looser and less deliberate. The figure group is not so tightly integrated. The ways in which the figures are painted in the two pictures present an interesting point of contrast. In the late picture the figures are not sharply delineated; they blend with the landscape and become an integral part of it. The figures in the Huntington picture, although painted with a wonderfully free and spirited brush, are (largely because of the spotlight effect upon them) existing more apart from the setting, which (from a visual point of view) they dominate. In the later painting the figures as an area of interest are effectively balanced against the light breaking through the tree trunks to the left. The basic organization of the picture lies in the sensitive play of these two areas of broken light against one another rather than the closely knit series of diagonals in the Huntington painting. Indeed the Huntington "Cottage Door" is unusual within Gainsborough's work in having such an emphatic and consistently developed compositional scheme. He normally prefers a more relaxed organization. But the situation is certainly not unique. Even within the Huntington collection Gainsborough's brilliant portrait of his close friend Karl Friedrich Abel has a composition worked out with equal care, and again dependent on a system of interlocking diagonals.

Although both "The Cottage Door" and Wilson's "River Scene with Bathers" are essentially imaginary landscapes, it is clear at once that they are meant to appeal to the spectator in different ways, and that the two painters are not attempting to evoke the same sort of response. Wilson's painting is laden with allusions to Italy, and to an ideal form of landscape, calm and idyllic, that is distant in both time and place from eighteenth-century England. Gainsborough's landscape is more rustic in tone and (at least for his contemporaries) appealed more in terms of their recollections of the local countryside than something remote and exotic. Furthermore, apart from the figures, much of the attraction in "The Cottage Door" lies in elements like the very gnarled old tree trunk, the textured thatch and wall of the cottage, and the glint of light on the stream. Gainsborough's contemporaries were aware of the differences involved in two such landscapes, just as they were aware of the different aesthetic responses evoked by Wilson's "Destruction of the Children of Niobe" and

"River Scene with Bathers." It is typical of the late eighteenth-century point of view that all three types of landscape (and some others as well) were accepted and enjoyed. Even as there were special names for Wilson's two modes, "the sublime" and "the beautiful," Gainsborough's "Cottage Door" would be referred to by most of his contemporaries as "picturesque." "The sublime" was concerned with excitement of an awesome and even terrifying kind; "the beautiful" dealt with calm, idyllic themes where all was serene and relaxed. "The picturesque" was not quite one or the other, and might even comprehend both. The word "picturesque" has almost as many different shades of meaning in eighteenth-century England as has the term "nature." In its broadest sense it meant simply those qualities in a scene or object that appealed to the eye of a painter, and looked well in painting, so that either beautiful or sublime objects could be picturesque. But, especially at the end of the century, the term was frequently used with a more specialized meaning. A pleasingly lively and irregular area of colors or light and shade was regarded as picturesque. Certain objects were thought more likely than others to produce these effects: gnarled old tree trunks; slightly dilapidated buildings; shaggy animals; generally anything that had rough textures and broken contours. The tree trunk and the cottage in "The Cottage Door" would be perfect examples of picturesque objects in this more specialized use of the term, as would the ragged clothing of the children, and the irregular, broken masses of foliage.

This "painterly-picturesque" interest was shared by many of Gainsborough's contemporaries, and finds one of its most complete realizations in the work of George Morland. Morland's paintings of domestic animals and barnyard scenes reveal a delight in exploring the play of light over various surfaces; the textures of fur, thatch, wood, straw all captured in free, virtuoso brushwork (*Fig. 82*).

Fig. 82. George Morland, *The Farmyard*, canvas, 39½ x 55 ins.

And yet it is entirely typical of the variety within the art of the period that while Morland was seeing animals in terms of light on surface, other artists were studying them with an almost clinical concern for anatomy and muscle structure. There is indeed a whole category of painting within Georgian art devoted to portraiture of animals (particularly horses), much of it of very high quality. Ben Marshall's painting of the racehorse Sam with the jockey Sam Chifney (*Fig. 83*) is an excellent example of the precision and sensitivity that was developed in this genre, a type of painting in which the nostalgia and sentiment that emerges from Gainsborough's depiction of the country and domestic animals have no part.

Although Gainsborough's contemporaries who thought about such matters would doubtless all agree in calling "The Cottage Door" picturesque, there would have been a lively discussion about exactly how this quality was achieved. For some critics the picturesque aspect would depend on the type of object Gainsborough had chosen to include in the picture; for others the object itself would be less important than the way in which Gainsborough had painted it. The tree trunk, for instance, might be considered picturesque because of its

Fig. 83. Ben Marshall, *Sam with Sam Chifney, Jr., Up*, canvas, 40 x 50 ins.

broken contours and rough textures, or because of the bold brush strokes and changing mosaic of colors with which the artist has chosen to depict it. This may sound like a rather empty argument which amounts to no more than six of one and half a dozen of the other. But in a broader context the point is of great interest for the history of art. According to the second interpretation, any object may be picturesque (that is, suitable for a picture) if it offers suitable stimulus to the eye of the painter in terms of light and color. The task of the artist and the function of the work of art is to communicate visual sensation rather than any subjective attitude; the ultimate purpose of the work as art is no longer regarded as ethical or moral, but simply to convey a heightened awareness of purely visual properties of light and color, a point of view that is usually associated with the Impressionists in the 1870's. Gainsborough's "Cottage Door" is, of course, a very long way from Impressionism and from an exclusive preoccupation with light and color. It is a painting permeated with a mood to which the effects of light and color are totally subject. But the way in which Gainsborough applies his pigment shows an interest in purely painterly and visual values which the more radical theorists of the picturesque (such as Richard Payne Knight) would immediately recognize as akin to their ideas.

[1]Bate Dudley, writing Gainsborough's obituary in *The Morning Herald* (London), 4 August 1788.

[2]Sir Joshua Reynolds, *Discourses on Art*, ed. Robert R. Wark (San Marino, Cal.), p. 250.

[3]*Somerset House Gazette*, I (March 1824), 348.

[4]Anon. *A Candid Review of the Exhibition* (London, 1780), p. 19.

Fig. 84. John Constable, *View on the Stour near Dedham*, canvas, 51 x 74 ins.

Chapter X

Constable's "View on the Stour near Dedham"

CONSTABLE's "View on the Stour near Dedham" represents a stretch of country for which the artist had deep affection. He was born within a couple of miles of the scene depicted and spent most of the first twenty years of his life within sight of the river, trees and buildings he includes in the painting. Although he lived much of his adult life in and around London, he returned again and again to this area of a few square miles as a source of inspiration for his art. His greatest achievement as a painter is a series of what may be called "portraits" of the Stour Valley in the immediate vicinity of Dedham. There is probably no other instance in the whole history of landscape painting of a major artist so passionately devoted to a particular geographical location. Even Cézanne's preoccupation with Mount Sainte-Victoire seems a passing flirtation by comparison.

Constable's section of the Stour Valley is not the sort of area that provokes a dramatic response. It is quiet country, rather flat and bounded at some distance by low-lying hills, and is only three or four miles away from a tidal estuary on the east coast of England. It is rich farming land, and the river Stour, wandering quietly through broad meadows, is one of the principal arteries traversing it. In the early seventeenth century the river was canalized through a series of locks and made navigable from Manningtree, at the head of the estuary, all the way to Sudbury, some thirty miles upstream. Barges were constantly moving up and down the river, usually pulled by horses that plodded along a towpath on one side of the stream, sometimes assisted by a sail if there was a favorable breeze, and constantly maneuvered by boys with poles and ropes. The region has not changed a great deal in the century and a half since Constable lived there. The Stour is no longer an important commercial artery, but it still meanders past open fields that remain relatively untouched by urban developments.

The specific view Constable has chosen for the Huntington picture is from the immediate vicinity of one of his father's properties, Flatford Mill, looking in a generally westerly direction upstream toward the village of Dedham, whose church tower is seen in the center distance. A couple of barges are being maneuvered near a lock on the river which was to the left, just beyond the view chosen by the artist. One of the tow horses stands idle on the far bank. In the middle distance, beyond the footbridge, another barge has its sail raised. The activity represented in the picture does not interfere with the general atmosphere of a quiet summer day with soft, fair-weather cumulus clouds moving up from the southwest across the sky. The mood of the painting is created to a great extent by Constable's subtly understood and beautifully conveyed sense of the light and atmosphere associated with a particular type of summer afternoon. But these sensations are skillfully sustained and reinforced by the pictorial organization: the broad arc of the river sweeping easily from the lower left around the fulcrum provided by the trees; the numerous diagonal accents enlivening without disturbing the stability created by the basic horizontals and verticals; the church tower punctuating the distant horizon with a gentle but palpable sense of focus and climax. Constable's concern, like that of Wilson, is basically with conveying a mood through landscape, but his means and the end desired are quite different. Constable's painting is a topographically accurate view of a particular place rather than something spun freely out of his imagination and recollections. The subjective sensations his paintings arouse are closely connected with specific, transitory effects of light and atmosphere. In these respects Wilson seems more generalized and idealized. Composition and arrangement are also important for Constable, but he is able to achieve the organization he wants without sacrificing geographical accuracy. The view as it appears on the canvas is close to what met Constable's eye as he stood on the edge of the Stour looking toward Dedham. He certainly takes some liberties, but these remain within a limited range of strong probabilities.

Like so many great works of art, Constable's "View on the Stour" has an ease and assurance that belie the patient deliberation and understanding that went into its creation. But Constable's development to the point when he could produce such a painting was a long and rather arduous one. The "View on the Stour" was painted in 1822 when the artist was forty-six, an age that would normally be considered as in mid-career. Constable had not, however, been in possession of the knowledge and ability to sustain his ideas over a canvas of this physical size for more than three or four years previous.

We do not now attach much importance to the actual dimensions of a work of art. A mural covering several hundred square feet is not necessarily better than a panel of as many square inches simply because it is bigger. But we are, perhaps, a little too glib in our thinking about such matters. Artistic quality certainly has very little to do with physical size, yet there are special skills and abilities involved in transferring artistic ideas from one dimension to another. Constable's ability to convey in paint those qualities that particularly attracted him about a landscape appeared first in small-scale drawings and sketches. His ideas were fully developed in these dimensions for about a decade before he succeeded in sustaining these sensations with equal force over a canvas the size of the Huntington "View on the Stour." There can be no doubt that whatever our feelings on the question may be now, he and his contemporaries attached considerable importance to this matter of size. Their thinking was to a great extent conditioned by the annual Royal Academy exhibition, which was a dominant and even a controlling factor in the activity of many artists. This exhibition, which was held each year beginning in May, was the major occasion of its kind in England. It was there that the established artists showed what they considered their most important works for the previous year, and it was there that aspiring artists competed for public attention and for the honors which the Academy had to bestow. These honors, election as associate of the Academy and ultimately as full academician, were dependent largely on the impression made at the exhibition. As these honors carried considerable prestige and professional recognition, most artists were eager to obtain them.

Constable was distinctly aware of the Academy and its exhibition, and much of his work as a mature artist was conditioned accordingly. In particular, at the end of the second decade of the nineteenth century he embarked on a series of what were for him very large paintings each measuring six by four and a half feet. He created six of these pictures between 1819 and 1825, exhibiting one at each Academy show for that period except 1823. They are in many respects the culmination of his art. There is little doubt that he himself regarded them as his most important works, on which he was prepared to rest his reputation as a landscapist. The paintings were created specifically with the exhibitions in mind. All six of the pictures represent views on the river Stour within two or three miles of each other. The first of these, "The White Horse," quickly brought Constable a degree of professional recognition he had been long denied, and he was elected an associate of the Academy in the autumn of 1819. The Huntington painting is the fourth of the series, exhibited in 1822.

The creation of these large canvases was for Constable an extremely exacting task on which he expended a considerable portion of each year. They were, of course, paintings developed in his studio in London, many miles away from the scenes they depicted. Constable knew the terrain around Dedham so well that he could no doubt have reconstructed the topography of each view entirely from his memory. But he had many notations and sketchbooks at hand. It seems probable that when composing the Huntington painting Constable turned back to a little sketchbook he had used eight years before during the summer of 1814. The book is only 3⅛ x 4¼ inches, so that the sketches are hardly more than miniatures in dimension, but they convey a remarkable amount of Constable's sensitivity to light and atmosphere. It is worth noting, however, that although at least three of the sketches are taken from practically the same viewpoint as the Huntington painting, none of them really anticipates the finished composition (*Figs. 85, 86 and 87*). Indeed it seems likely that in order to obtain the grouping of elements that satisfied him, Constable opened his angle of vision a little wider than normal. The group of trees on the left and the house on the right that enframe the view in the painting do not both appear in any one of the sketches. There is, of course, no reason to suppose that Constable originally made these sketches with paintings in mind. On the contrary, there seems every reason to believe that the 1814 and other similar sketchbooks he kept more as diaries, notations of things and effects seen, jotted down as much for the pleasure of the moment as for future reference.

In working up one of his exhibition paintings Constable might also refer to the little oil sketches that form a particularly appealing facet of his art. These, although considerably larger than the pencil drawings in the sketchbooks, are still of small physical dimensions, about seven by ten inches being an average size (*Fig. 88*). It was in these paintings that Constable's ideas about landscape first matured, a decade or more before the large exhibition canvases such as "View on the Stour." These oil sketches have a freedom and breadth of handling, a freshness of color, and a plein-air sense of atmosphere that gives them a strong and immediate appeal. The great majority of them were painted out of doors in the presence of the motif they depict, and they reflect this immediacy and directness. They reveal more clearly than any other facet of Constable's art his preoccupation with the changing moods of his native countryside as seen through light and atmosphere, a preoccupation thoroughly characteristic of the romantic period to which he belongs. To modern eyes, conditioned by landscape painting of the late-nineteenth and early-twentieth century, these vigorous little sketches appear complete, self-contained works of art. But there is no evidence they were so regarded by Constable himself. Rather they were, like the sketchbooks, personal records of things seen, which might or might not be referred to in composing works for sale or exhibition.

There is no small oil sketch known that was directly involved in Constable's development of the Huntington painting, but there is an important large-scale sketch that was clearly the immediate predecessor of the finished canvas (*Fig. 89*). This sketch is for practical purposes the same size as the Huntington landscape and was intended as a means by which Constable could work out his general effects at full scale. As far as we know now, it was in connection with the earliest of his "six foot" canvases, "The White Horse," exhibited in 1819, that Constable first employed a full-sketch, and he continued to use them for several of the others in this major series of views on the river Stour. It is an idea that has practically no precedent in the history of art. Small-scale preparatory sketches are commonplace, but full-size studies for large paintings are virtually

Fig. 85, 86, 87. John Constable, *Three Pages from the 1814 Sketchbook*, pencil, 3⅛ x 4½ ins. (The Victoria and Albert Museum, London).

Fig. 88. John Constable, *Barges on the Stour*, oil on paper, 10¼ x 12¼ ins. (The Victoria and Albert Museum, London).

Fig. 89. John Constable, *View on the Stour*, canvas, 51 x 75¼ ins. (The Royal Holloway College).

unknown. Constable's use of the device underlines the importance he attached to the great exhibition canvases such as "View on the Stour," and the need he must have felt for special aids when working on a physically large painting.

It is fascinating to compare the sketch and finished picture in some detail, for the juxtaposition provides valuable insight into Constable's aims and practices. The sketch is very much more broadly and freely painted. The various forms, especially the trees and foliage, are treated in a much more generalized fashion; the clouds also are not so particularized. In order to prevent a heavy, opaque effect in the broadly painted dark shadows Constable has flecked the surface with lighter pigment. All of these sketch-like qualities are particularly attractive to us today. But there can be no doubt, as we explore the comparison further, concerning the thoughtful deliberation and sensitivity that motivated the changes adopted in the finished version. Constable himself comments on the changes he has made in a letter to a close friend: "I have taken away the sail, and added another barge in the middle of the picture, with a principal figure, altered the group of trees, and made the bridge entire. The picture has now a rich center, and the right-hand side becomes only an accessory."[1] This is certainly not a complete inventory of the changes, but it gives an indication of the direction of Constable's thinking. The change in the sail was made in the sketch itself. The large barge in the middle ground originally had a sail, the outline of which can still be clearly seen under the paint depicting the trees. A much more trivial but still significant alteration involved lowering the distant sail so that it leads the eye toward the church tower rather than competing with it as a focal point. The development of the "rich center" of the picture has been handled with care. It is achieved not only by the addition of another barge and figure, but by the elimination of distractions around the periphery. The man rowing the boat on the left margin of the sketch has gone, as have the couple fishing in the lower right. The latter group, curiously small in scale in the sketch, would have proved a considerable attraction to the eye if fully developed in the finished painting; instead an eel spear and a moored fishing boat both provide diagonal accents directing our attention toward the central area. It is interesting to note, as other students have pointed out, that for the added barge and its active figure Constable turned again to one of his early sketchbooks, this one from 1813, where he recorded this precise motif in a tiny thumbnail drawing (*Figs. 90 and 91*).

The heightening of the forward tree gives greater dignity to the grove and a stronger verticality to this fulcrum around which swings the broad arc of the river. But the important change in the trees is in the much greater particularization of the limb structure and foliage. It is probable that Constable here again made reference to earlier detailed studies. He made several large-scale drawings of trees in 1817, paying careful attention not so much to masses of foliage as to the organic relationship of the branches and the growth pattern (*Figs. 92 and*

Fig. 90. John Constable, *Man Poling a Barge*, pencil, 3½ x 4¾ ins. (The Victoria and Albert Museum, London).

Fig. 91. John Constable, *View on the Stour near Dedham*, (detail).

93); and it is just these qualities that distinguish the trees in the finished painting from the broadly blocked out areas of foliage in the oil sketch. There is not, however, any drawing now known that is specifically connected with the group of trees in the Huntington painting.

A similar distinction exists between the treatment of the clouds in the two pictures. In the sketch Constable is more concerned with general effects of light, shadow, and movement than with the detailed construction of clouds. We know that in 1821 and 1822 Constable was particularly preoccupied with observation of clouds and it was in these years that he produced a whole series of small oil sketches devoted predominantly, and frequently exclusively, to studies of the sky. In a letter of October 1821, written when he was already deeply involved with the creation of the Huntington picture, Constable speaks at some length about his attitude toward the sky in landscape painting: "It will be difficult to name a class of landscape in which sky is not the keynote, the standard of scale, and the chief organ of sentiment. . . . The sky is the source of light in Nature, and governs everything; even our common observations on the weather of the day are altogether suggested by it."[2] Constable's cloud studies are frequently inscribed with specific data concerning the conditions under which they were painted. One, for instance, in the National Gallery of Victoria, Melbourne (*Fig. 94*), is inscribed "5th of September, 1822, 10 o'clock, morning, looking south-east, brisk wind at west. Very bright and fresh grey clouds running over a yellow bed, about half way in the sky. Very appropriate to the 'coast at Osmington'." It is this highly specific sort of observation of the sky that Constable has incorporated in the finished version of "View on the Stour." And there can be little doubt that it is the sky and the particular quality of light emanating from it that are so important in creating the overall mood projected from the painting.

Thus if the finished painting lacks some of the breadth of handling and bravura that modern taste finds appealing in the sketch, the final product has many impressive, positive qualities of its own. In particular it gives evidence in all its parts of thoughtful and sensitive deliberation concerning how best to achieve and intensify those qualities for which Constable was striving. The canvas is a quietly triumphant statement of the artist's whole philosophy of landscape. And yet the artist was uneasy and nervous when he at last sent the painting off to the Academy exhibition. "I never worked so hard before," he wrote to his friend Archdeacon Fisher in April 1822, "it wanted much — but still I hope the work in it is better than any I have got done."[3]

The painting received a rather lukewarm reception from the press when the exhibition opened, but at least it was not ignored. Some critics complained of Constable's lack of variety in subject matter (this was the fourth large view along the river Stour that he had exhibited in as many years). The writer for the *Museum*, although he felt the picture "wanted breadth" considered it

Fig. 92. John Constable, *Elm Trees in Old Hall Park, East Bergholt*, pencil and wash, 23¼ x 19½ ins. (The Victoria and Albert Museum, London).

Fig. 93. John Constable, *View on the Stour near Dedham*, (detail).

Fig. 94. John Constable, *Cloud Study*, canvas, 12 x 18 ins. (The National Gallery of Victoria, Melbourne).

almost, if not quite, the best landscape in the exhibition. The critic for the *Examiner* was warmer, finding in "View on the Stour" the consoling recollection of the charm of nature amid the surrounding glare of gold frames and gaudy color.[4] The painting did not, however, obtain for Constable the election as full academician which he wished for. He had to wait another seven years, until 1829, for that honor.

But the Royal Academy show of 1822 was by no means the only public appearance of "View on the Stour." Another more exciting and important event took place when the painting was among three by Constable exhibited at the Paris Salon in 1824. Constable had enjoyed a considerable reputation in France among both dealers and artists for some time. Géricault had seen "The Hay Wain" in London in 1821 and spoke with great enthusiasm of the painting to Delacroix. A French art dealer with the English-sounding name of John Arrowsmith began importing Constable's paintings into France and he was followed shortly afterward by a colleague, Claude Schroth. After a certain amount of wrangling over price, Arrowsmith capped his activities by buying both "The Hay Wain" and "View on the Stour" from Constable in April of 1824 at £250 for the pair, with a small view of Yarmouth thrown in. In May Constable had the paintings ready to send to Paris, and he remarks in a letter to Fisher, with a touch of chauvinism and possibly a little nostalgia, "Think of the lovely valleys mid the peacefull farm houses of Suffolk forming a scene of exhibition to amuse the gay & frivolous Parisians."[5] In June Constable learned of the safe arrival of the paintings in Paris, where they were first seen at the gallery of Arrowsmith. Later in the year they were exhibited at the Louvre. In December Constable again wrote to Fisher in high spirits, "My Paris affairs go on very well . . . though the Director (the Count Forbain) gave [my pictures] very respectable situations [in the Louvre] in the first instance, yet on their being exhibited a few weeks, they so greatly advanced in reputation that they were removed from their original situations to a post of honour, two prime places . . . in the principal room. I am much indebted to the artists for this alarum in my praise; but I will do justice to the Count. He is no artist (I believe) and he thought 'as the colours are rough, they must be seen at a distance.' They found their mistake as they then acknowledged the richness of the texture, and attention to the surface of objects. . . . They call out much about their vivacity and freshness, a thing unknown to their own paintings."[6] The climax of this acclaim came at the end of the year when Charles X awarded Constable a gold medal for the merit of his landscapes, an honor that gave great pleasure to the painter, although he could not be persuaded to go to Paris to receive it in person. An electrotype of the medal has been set into the frame of the Huntington painting.

Constable himself puts his finger on what the French artists most admired when he says that they are struck with the vivacity, freshness, and richness of texture of his works. Delacroix, the most important and most vocal of the French painters who extolled Constable's pictures, was attracted by precisely these qualities. Constable's general philosophy of landscape as embodied in "View on the Stour" affected him not at all. But he was fascinated by the broken colors and vigorous brushwork that enlivened the paint surface in contrast to the tight enamel-like textures of most French painting at the time. Delacroix paid Constable the highest of compliments by repainting parts of his own exhibit at the 1824 Salon, "The Massacre at Chios," to incorporate some of the Englishman's livelier sense of color and surface. It was not, however, until the rise of the Barbizon school a decade or more later that Constable's attitude toward landscape, as distinct from his technique, began to make much of an impression on French painting.

"View on the Stour" seems to have remained in France for about six years. We do not know the subsequent history of the painting in detail, but it was in the sale of a Parisian painter, Amable-Paul Coutan, in April of 1830. Presumably then or shortly after, it returned to England to enter the collection of W. Carpenter of the British Museum, in whose collection it was when engraved in 1845 by W. R. Smith. Carpenter sold the painting to Thomas Miller of Preston, and following his death in 1860 it passed to his son T. Horrocks Miller. It was sold by the trustees of that gentleman's estate in 1925, passing through the hands of the dealers Agnew and Joseph Duveen before being acquired by Mr. Huntington in May of the same year. It is by far the most impressive landscape in the Huntington collection, and among the major achievements in the history of European landscape painting.

[1] Quoted from R. B. Beckett, *John Constable and the Fishers* (London, 1952), pp. 93-4.

[2] Ibid. 82.

[3] Ibid. 91.

[4] Quoted from William T. Whitley, *Art in England 1821-1837* (New York, 1930), p. 29.

[5] Beckett, op. cit. 164.

[6] Ibid. 199.

Fig. 95. J. M. W. Turner, *Grand Canal, Venice*, canvas, 58¼ x 43½ ins.

Chapter XI

Turner's "Grand Canal, Venice"

THE NAMES OF TURNER AND CONSTABLE are frequently paired, as are those of Reynolds and Gainsborough. Reynolds and Gainsborough were the leading portraitists of the late eighteenth century; Turner and Constable were the foremost landscapists of the first half of the nineteenth. In both instances the juxtaposition has the useful function of sharpening, by comparison, our understanding of each artist in the pair. Although Turner and Constable have a great deal in common, and share many basic attitudes toward landscape and nature, they place the emphasis differently. For instance, whereas Constable was never tempted to leave England, and devoted his career to an intense study of a few areas of his native land, Turner roamed over Europe, constantly searching for exciting motifs to paint. Constable's art is founded on close empirical observation of effects of light and atmosphere. Turner adds to this a constant and often quite self-conscious awareness of the whole European tradition of landscape painting, on which he frequently calls to enrich his own work. Constable's attitude toward nature is relatively humble and self-effacing; Turner appears more aggressive, orchestrating his treatment of a motif in a much more apparent fashion in order to achieve a desired effect. Even in the development of their professional careers the men pose an interesting contrast. Constable was a slow starter, and was in his thirties before he painted anything of real distinction. He was forty-three when elected an associate of the Royal Academy, and fifty-two before gaining the status of a full academician. Turner, just one year older than Constable, was exhibiting at the Academy before he was twenty, and was elected a full academician when only twenty-seven. Constable's active career as a painter was about thirty years; Turner's was nearly twice that. In their own day Turner's reputation overshadowed that of Constable. Certainly this is no longer the case, and most well-informed critics today would find it difficult (and essentially irrelevant) to rank the two artists in order of merit.

Turner is not so strongly represented in the Huntington collection as Constable. "View on the Stour" is one of Constable's major works and embodies in one way or another most of what he set out to accomplish as a landscape painter. This cannot honestly be said of "The Grand Canal, Venice," the most important painting by Turner in the collection. But it is in many respects a characteristic work that reveals a good deal about the artist. It is a bustling and rather opulent picture, especially in comparison with "View on the Stour." If we are defining our terms very sharply and narrowly "The Grand Canal" is hardly a landscape at all. The primary objects depicted are buildings, people, boats and water, rather than land and what grows upon it. It is a "cityscape," a view of one of the most remarkable and spectacular cities of Europe. We are looking along a stretch of the Grand Canal, the principal artery of Venice. Stately palaces of the great Venetian families line the watercourse, and in the distance, spanning the canal, is the Rialto bridge, one of the most famous and distinctive structures in the city. The scene is thronged with people, in rich and brightly colored costumes, all crowded on the narrow quays that border the canal. The canal itself is dotted with boats, many with sails raised, adding to the visual excitement of the scene. The city is bathed in dazzling sunlight under an intense blue sky, flecked with light cirrus clouds. The impression of busy, urban activity is in sharp contrast to the quiet repose of the Stour valley.

The effect is created not only by what Turner has represented but also by the way in which he has organized his picture. He chooses a vertical format, thereby minimizing the stabilizing effect of a long horizon line. The dominant accents in the painting are diagonals: the shimmering water leading from the lower right to the Rialto; the roof lines of the buildings leading to the same area from the upper right, reinforced by the ladder-like cloud formation. Against these are played the verticals of the buildings themselves which loom up with a height and abruptness that are also disquieting.

Turner does not allow the eye to come to rest on any focal or climactic point. Not only are we distracted by all the coming and going of the great throng of people, but also (on a more abstract level) our eye moves uneasily back and forth between the large, glistening palace that dominates the right half of the picture and the distant Rialto toward which so many accents lead in the left background. Underlining this relationship is the church tower, in the mathematical center of the picture, punctuating the path along which our eye is constantly moving from the heavy roof-cornice of the palace to the Rialto. Students have frequently criticized the painting because of this tense, unresolved effect it creates. But if we turn to a consideration of the various circumstances surrounding the picture, and its position in Turner's career, we may find evidence to suggest that he created this effect intentionally.

Turner exhibited "The Grand Canal" at the Royal Academy in 1837 (which, it so happens, was also the year of Constable's death). Turner had been exhibiting at the Academy for forty-seven years and would continue to do so until 1850. The painting is thus a mature work from the latter part of the artist's career, although the pigment has not yet taken on the evanescent and opalescent qualities that are now so much admired in his pictures from the 1840's. The Huntington painting is the sixth in a series of twenty-five concerned with

Venice that Turner exhibited between 1833 and 1846. The city had a fascination for him that reminds one a little of Constable's preoccupation with the Stour Valley, although Venice was only one of a great many amorous attachments for Turner. He must have been enchanted by the concentration of color and light in the Venetian scene, factors that became the dominant and controlling considerations in his later work. Venice may also have had a symbolic significance for him; a great city in decay, reflecting the transitory nature of empire. For Venice was already in Turner's day stripped of its once vast commercial strength, and had become simply a haunt of tourists. He visited the city certainly on two and probably on three occasions. The first time was late in 1819, when he made a great many pencil sketches of the area. He was probably there again in 1833.[1] The last visit was in the late summer of 1840. In 1820 and 21, shortly after the initial first-hand contact with Venice, Turner made three exhibition watercolors of Venetian views. But students have always been puzzled by the fact that he waited fourteen years before producing his first oil painting of the city. While it is not possible to offer any convincing explanation for Turner's long delay in taking up a subject which he subsequently found so appealing, it has been suggested by several students that what attracted him to the theme in the early 1830's was work he was then doing illustrating books in which Venice and Italy figured prominently. In 1830 he was making drawings for Byron's *Childe Harold*, and was sufficiently impressed to develop a painting which he exhibited in 1832 under the title "Childe Harold's Pilgrimage — Italy." At the same time he was also working on vignettes illustrating the poems of Samuel Rogers, and Venetian scenes figured in two of these. Doubtless his visit to the city in 1833 fanned the flame further.

When Turner came to develop the Huntington painting in 1837 it was not to any sketches from his recent trip that he turned for guidance, but to drawings made on his first visit in 1819. The source from which he worked is almost certainly an opening from his so-called "Milan to Venice" sketchbook (*Figs. 96 and 97*). Interestingly enough this same drawing provided the source for one of the watercolors of Venice which Turner made in 1820 and 1821 after his return from the early trip (*Fig. 98*). The three renditions of the motif make an instructive comparison. The pencil sketch is, of course, the only one actually made on the spot; the other two were worked up in London. The watercolor reproduces pretty much the whole of the composition of the drawing; the painting is developed from only the right two-thirds. The most striking differences are in proportion. In the watercolor the apparent width of the Grand Canal is drastically reduced, the buildings appear relatively much higher, the Rialto much closer, and the general effect much more confined. In the painting the Rialto is pushed further back into the distance, and the canal is broadened to assume more closely the proportions and distance suggested by the drawing; but vertically at least there is a wide-angle-vision effect that strongly accents

Figs. 96 and 97. J. M. W. Turner, *Two adjoining pages from Turner's 1819 Milan to Venice Sketchbook,* pencil (The British Museum, London).

the apparent height of the buildings in the right foreground. Also our angle of vision seems to be from a point close to the right side of the canal.

Turner's facility in developing convincing architectural detail in the water-color and oil from his pencil squiggles is very impressive. But he is clearly not concerned with precise topographical accuracy in either of the pictures he derived from the sketch. Of particular interest is his treatment of the Palazzo Grimani, the large building that dominates the right side of the painting. In the oil he moves it forward relative to its neighbors so that it appears noticeably more massive than in the sketch or the watercolor. At the same time he is at considerable pains to preserve a curious eccentricity that actually exists in the building. The corner towards us is not in fact square, but a slightly acute angle,

Fig. 98. J. M. W. Turner, *Grand Canal, Venice,* watercolor, 11 x 15½ ins. (Kurt F. Pantzer, Indianapolis).

which makes the cornice line appear to slope too sharply in perspective. This is a detail that attracted Turner's attention when he made his first pencil sketch, and which he retained in both the watercolor and the oil. Interestingly enough it was also a detail that caught the attention of Ruskin, whose father purchased the painting from Turner shortly after it was exhibited. The younger Ruskin checked out this matter on his visit to Venice in 1851 and wrote back to his father explaining that the palace "was not square, but that the corner was an acute angle — built in necessity in consequence of the direction of the canal. Turner's perspective is therefore perfectly right."[2]

But if Turner is punctilious in this respect, in others he allowed himself considerable latitude. The church tower he moves around to suit his composition. Also the number of buildings along the canal between the Grimani Palace and the Rialto is treated in a flexible fashion depending on the sense of distance he wishes to create. And, of course, all the accessory items — the quays, the boats, the people — are entirely of Turner's own creation, although with obvious attention to what is appropriate for the scene.

In the Huntington painting the people are a very important part of the picture. Not only do their rich costumes add great color and variety, but we are also immediately concerned about the actions and activity that are taking place. Turner's intentions here were quite specific. When he exhibited the painting he appended to the catalog listing a couple of lines from Shakespeare's *Merchant of Venice*:

III, iii *Antonio* Hear me yet, good Shylock.
       Shylock I'll have my bond.

This reference has puzzled and even irritated many critics from the time the picture was first exhibited down to the present. It is only after a rather diligent search that we locate the bald-headed man along the lower right margin of the painting who leans out of a window, holding a paper, a knife, and measuring

Fig. 99. J. M. W. Turner,
Grand Canal, Venice, (detail)

scales (*Fig. 99*). This, apparently, must be Shylock, and Antonio must be one
of the two figures in the extreme right foreground. On the face of it this seems
a very perverse way to handle the ostensible "subject" of the picture. It appears
like an afterthought stuck in. One of the critics of the day said, rather truthfully,
that Shylock looked for all the world like Mr. Punch popping out of his box.
There is no point in attempting to rationalize and justify Turner's curious
treatment of this episode. But there is equally no reason to doubt his sincerity in
incorporating it in his picture. Everything we know about the man's attitude
toward the subjects of his paintings supports the contention that he would not
be acting flippantly in this matter.

Turner is indeed probably the last major landscapist who supported the idea
that landscape painting could and should be the vehicle for presenting grand
themes from history and literature; that it should be an art of mind and emotion,
not merely sensuous perception. In this respect it has been correctly pointed
out that he is one of the most traditional landscapists of his generation. Modern
critics who look at all of his paintings simply as pure landscape and ignore the
literary allusions he frequently added to them miss a dimension of Turner's art
that had great importance for him and his contemporaries. He would occasionally write verses himself and append them to the title of a painting in order to
enrich and supplement the mood and associations he wished to create. Passages
from poets such as Thomson and Byron were also frequently added to the
titles for his landscapes. But he treated these sources with the same liberty he
did his own topographical pencil sketches; they were the springboard, but no
more than that, from which his visual imagination soared. Indeed this "poetic"
attitude toward landscape is one of the key factors that freed him from any
literal dependence on a motif and prepared the way for the most spectacular
of his later paintings.

In considering the Shakespearean reference in the Huntington painting it is worth noting that another allusion, this time to *Romeo and Juliet*, appeared in the Venetian subject Turner exhibited the preceding year at the Academy (*Fig. 100*). The earlier picture, entitled "Juliet and her Nurse," is a nocturnal scene of St. Mark's Square with the church and campanile in the background, viewed from a vantage point on the roofs at the southwest angle of the area. Here, as in the Huntington picture, the ostensible subject is rather incidentally placed in the lower right corner of the painting. And of course, as the critics were quick to point out, Juliet and her nurse had no business being in Venice at all. Shakespeare set his play in Verona.

But "Juliet and her Nurse" is essentially a mood picture, and the magical light bathing this nocturnal scene evokes a sensation akin to that of Shakespeare's great love-tragedy. This is the way in which most critics from Ruskin on have interpreted the painting, passing over as irrelevant the casual and inaccurate way in which the ostensible subject is introduced. The mood of the Huntington painting is very different, suggesting the full blaze of high noon in a glittering and bustling commercial city. But it is a mood that may have as much to do with *The Merchant of Venice* as that of "Juliet and her Nurse" has to do with *Romeo and Juliet*.

Fig. 100. J. M. W. Turner, *Juliet and Her Nurse*, canvas, 36 x 48 ins. (Mrs. Flora Whitney Miller, New York)

Turner was certainly responsive to a great variety of moods and sensations. The contrast between Venice at night and Venice at noon is of just the type that would appeal to him both visually (in terms of light and color) and emotionally. And it is entirely characteristic of him to intensify these moods by allusions to literature. Turner's delight in this type of variety and range of emotion is typical of the age in which he lived, and his art exemplifies this outlook to a remarkable degree. This contention is well exemplified by the four paintings he exhibited at the academy in 1837. In addition to "The Grand Canal" these were: "Apollo and Daphne" (*Fig. 101*), "The Parting of Hero and Leander" (*Fig. 102*), and "Snow-storm, Avalanche and Inundation" (*Fig. 103*). "Apollo and Daphne" is an idyllic scene evoking the quiet, spacious Italian countryside, a balanced composition presenting a view up an extensive valley, enframed with hills and trees; a picture in the same general tradition as Wilson's "River Scene with Bathers." "Hero and Leander" is a more tempestuous affair; a nocturnal scene with a turbulent sky, dramatic lighting and a strange imaginary accumulation of classical temples clinging to a steep hillside. The "Snow-storm" is a great swirl of light and color engulfing and almost dissolving the mountains and human figures that are just discernible. It is safe to say that no landscapist prior to Turner could command (or indeed would wish to command) such a range of emotion in his art. And this quality had been a salient feature of Turner's painting since the beginning of the century. As early as 1803, for instance, he exhibited his famous "Calais Pier" (*Fig. 104*) alongside "The Festival at Macon" (*Fig. 105*); the first is a scene of the utmost turbulence, skilfully compounded from personal observation and from recollections of Dutch seventeenth-century seascapes; the second is a highly successful essay, essentially reminiscent of the idyllic calm of Claude Lorrain. The juxtaposition was intended to demonstrate Turner's control over the expressive possibilities of landscape, and the range of emotion he could evoke. In his earlier work, up to about 1830, much of this variety was obtained by employing, with significant modification, stylistic devices developed by his great predecessors in European landscape painting, particularly of the seventeenth century. In the later part of his career these reminiscences of earlier artists became less obvious. The desire for variety and range in emotional expression remained but was obtained in a more abstract and original way through Turner's extraordinary evocations of light and color. This late phase of Turner's work, which is so greatly admired in the mid-twentieth century, was already developing at the time he painted "The Grand Canal" in the Huntington collection. Indications of this direction are found in the shimmering light that dissolves some of the surface detail of the buildings ranged along the Grand Canal, and in the generally high-keyed color, intensified by the white ground layer over which Turner builds his pigment. But it is much less apparent in the Huntington picture than in, for instance, the "Snow-storm" exhibited in the same year. The relatively conservative character

Fig. 101. J. M. W. Turner, *Apollo and Daphne*, panel, 42½ x 77½ ins.
(The Tate Gallery, London).

Fig. 102. J. M. W. Turner, *The Parting of Hero and Leander*, canvas,
57½ x 93 ins. (The National Gallery, London).

Fig. 103. J. M. W. Turner, *Snowstorm, Avalanche and
Inundation*, canvas, 36 x 48¼ ins. (The Art Institute
of Chicago).

Fig. 104. J. M. W. Turner, *Calais Pier*, canvas, 67¾ x 94½ ins. (The National Gallery, London).

Fig. 105. J. M. W. Turner, *Festival of the Vintage, Macon*, canvas, 57 x 92 ins. (Graves Art Gallery, Sheffield).

of the "Grand Canal" is all the more puzzling in view of the fact that Venice was one of the themes that seems to have stimulated Turner in the development of his late work, or at least that he found most congenial. A watercolor indicates what Venice might become through his eyes (*Fig. 106*). The elements in the view, the buildings, boats and water, have all but dissolved into a shimmering colored mist, and the colors themselves are of an opalescent character that further enhances the transitory, evanescent effect. Turner's preoccupation is entirely with light and color, to the exclusion of almost every other aspect of the motif. He is abstracting from the view simply those sensations that interest him, showing no concern for many others. It is an attitude that leads to pictures with a strong resemblance to various phases of mid twentieth-century art; and of course such willingness to abstract from a motif a few sensations is essentially a modern outlook. But the retention of a clear reference to a specific location, and the concern with evoking a mood derived from that location, both exemplify general attitudes toward landscape that are characteristic of Turner's own day, and link even these late works (although somewhat tenuously) with the outlook of men such as Constable.

The Huntington view of the Grand Canal is much more clearly within the normal range of early nineteenth-century landscape painting. The conscious evocation of mood through literary association as well as visual sensation is particularly characteristic of the "romantic" outlook. But the concern with light and color, heightened and intensified by the Venetian environment, point in the direction of Turner's later works.

Turner's art (at least until 1840) is the most complete and impressive embodiment of the attitude mapped out in the introductory chapter to this book. In his work, more than that of any other British painter, the aspirations of the romantic period toward universality of expression rise to the level of great art. He is in full control of an extraordinary repertory of styles and modes, and can range with ease and conviction through the whole gamut of sensation. In these respects the only other painter of the age who equals and in some respects excells him is the Spaniard, Goya.

But Turner's achievement builds very clearly on the work of earlier artists, not only in the pictorial forms he employs but also in his ability to move with sureness from one stylistic vocabulary to another. The desire for variety in expression and the exploration of means to achieve it are things we have watched developing in earlier chapters. Hogarth, although basically a rococo artist, was trying (as early as the second quarter of the eighteenth century) to extend the range of expression possible in that style. Reynolds and Wilson, by the 1760's, had developed the idea of borrowing stylistic devices from various earlier artists, and consciously playing on our associations with the art of other times and places as means of enlarging the emotional content of their art. Lawrence and Constable in the next generation adopted less blatant, more

Fig. 106. J. M. W. Turner, *Mouth of the Grand Canal*, watercolor, 8¼ x 12¼ ins. (Mr. and Mrs. Paul Mellon).

subtle means toward similar ends. Lawrence was able to manipulate the poses of his sitters and the arrangements of his compositions in order to characterize strikingly different people. Constable studied effects of light and atmosphere to suggest the rich variety in the moods of his native countryside. Even Gainsborough, from a stylistic point of view the most consistent and traditional of the artists considered, shared to a limited degree this interest in emotional contrasts, especially in his later work. Furthermore, his utilization of the reference to Van Dyck in "The Blue Boy," and his exploration of qualities associated with the picturesque in "The Cottage Door" are typical of other early romantic interests. Turner understood and exploited all these possibilities; no device developed by the romantic artists was unknown to or unused by him.

Turner is thus a product of his own age. And yet those students of modern art who see him as an important forerunner of late nineteenth and twentieth-century attitudes are also right in their estimate. For the romantic period is an essential prelude to modern art. The rococo style of the mid-eighteenth century might be viewed as a playful coda, bringing to an end the magnificent epoch that began in the fifteenth century and continued with a great procession of style phases through the sixteenth and seventeenth. The romantic period admired this tradition, and no artist of importance at that time was unaware of the debt he owed to the giants of the sixteenth and seventeenth centuries. But the romantics wanted more than their immediate inheritance provided. With this widening interest went a subtle but fundamental change in attitude toward art. The Renaissance idea that saw art as ultimately ethical and moral, elevating the thoughts and actions of the spectator, was never discarded. Yet along with this came an increasing concern with art as sensation. A function of the artist was to communicate clarified and intensified sensations which might or might not have anything to do with the Renaissance objective. This new freedom and universality of intention paved the way for experiments in art during the late nineteenth century. Thus the romantic period, although it has a distinct personality of its own, is also one of the great watersheds in the history of European art, for it is during this century that the Renaissance ideals are transformed into the foundations of modern art.

[1]See Hardy George "Turner in Venice" *The Art Bulletin*, LIII (1971), 84-87.

[2]*Ruskin's Letters from Venice*, ed. John Lewis Bradley (New Haven, 1955), p. 16.

Index

Abel, Karl Friedrich, 75, 106, *Fig. 57*
Academy, Royal, London, 43, 45, 47, 62-63, 64, 104, 113, 118, 120, 123, 124
Adam, Robert, 9, *Figs. 9-12*
Agnew (art dealer), 64, 121
Aristotle, 49
Arrowsmith, John, 120
association (in art), 8, 13

Bach, Johann Christian, 75, *Fig. 57*
Baker, C. H. Collins, 40, 49
Barbizon school, 121
Baron, Bernard, 26, *Fig. 25*
Barrett, Edward, 59
Barrett, Elizabeth, 59
Barrett, Judith, 59, 62
Barrett, Samuel, 59
Barry, James, 43-44, 55, 82, 83-86, 90, *Figs. 63-65*
Bath, Somerset, 31, 45
Beale, Mary, 27
beautiful (according to Burke), 86, 107
Beechey, William, 60, 63
Bernini, Gian Lorenzo, 69
bitumen, 56
Blake, William, Ch. VII *passim*, 5, *Figs. 59, 60, 66, 68*
Blessington, Lady, 64-65, *Fig. 47*
Boaden, James, 47, 49, 52
Boitard, François, 73
Boitard, Louis-Philippe, 73, *Fig. 52*
Boucher, François, 4, *Fig. 1*
Bowden (country house), 7, *Fig. 7*
Boydell, John, 80
Brandoin, Charles, 73, *Fig. 53*
Brendel, Otto J., 13
British Museum, 67
Browning, Elizabeth Barrett, 63
Bunbury, Henry William, 68
Burke, Edmund, 45, 84-86
Buttall, Jonathan, Ch. III *passim*
Byron, Lord, 125, 128

Calonne, C. A. de, 56
Campbell, Thomas, 45, 46

Carpenter, W., 121
Carracci, Agostino, 68
Catalani, Mme., 75, *Fig. 56*
Cézanne, Paul, 111
Cincinnati Museum, 105
Charles X, King of France, 120
Charlotte, Queen, 45, 60
Constable, John, Ch. X *passim*, 12, 90, 123, 124-125, 132, 133, *Figs. 85-88, 90, 92*
   "The Hay Wain," 120
   "View on the Stour near Dedham," Ch. X *passim*, 123, *Figs. 84, 89, 91, 93*
   "The White Horse," 113
conversation piece portraits, 16-18
Coram, Capt. Thomas, 18-20, *Fig. 17*
Coutan, Amable-Paul, 121
Cruikshank, Isaac, 68

Dartmouth, Earl of, 94
Davis, Gilbert, 67
Delacroix, Eugene, 120, 121
Derby, Countess of, 60
Desenfans, Noel Joseph, 56-57
Devis, Arthur, 16, *Fig. 15*
Dighton, Robert, 68
Dulwich College, 57
Duveen, Joseph, 39, 40-41, 57, 64, 121

Edwards, Edward, 30, 39

Farington, Joseph, 30-31, 38-39
Farren, Elizabeth, later Countess of Derby, 60
Fisher, Archdeacon, 118, 120
Flaxman, John, 5, 86-90, *Fig. 67*
Fonthill Abbey, 7, *Fig. 8*
Forbain, Count, 120
Fox, Charles James, 45
Fuseli, Henry, 5, 32, 80, 82, 83, 90, *Figs. 3, 62*

Gainsborough, Thomas, Chs. III and IX *passim*, 5, 7, 12, 60, 64, 123, 133, *Fig. 6*

"Karl Friedrich Abel," 106
"The Blue Boy," Ch. III *passim*, 64,
133, *Figs. 26, 31, 32*
"Hon. Edward Bouverie," 32, *Fig. 30*
"The Cottage Door," Ch. IX *passim*,
41, *Figs. 76-81*
"Hon. Frances Duncombe," 32
"Lady Margaret Fordyce," 32
"Hon. Mrs. Graham," 32
"Lady with a Spaniel," 31, *Fig. 27*
Lord and Lady Ligonier, 39
"Paul Cobb Methuen," 32
"Lady Petre," 31, *Fig. 28*
Garrick, David, 34, 44
Garter, Order of, 15, 18, 26
Gascoigne family, 16, *Fig. 14*
George III, 45
George, Dorothy, 67
George, Prince of Wales, 45
Géricault, Théodore, 120
Ghezzi, Pier Leone, 69-71
Gibbon, Edward, 45
Gillray, James, 5, 58, 82
Goldsmith, Oliver, 101
Goya, Francisco José de, 133
Grimani Palace, 127
Grosvenor, Earl, 39

Hastings, Warren, 64-65, *Fig. 46*
Haward, Francis, 56, *Fig. 42*
Hayman, Francis, 16, 34, *Fig. 14*
Henderson, John, 67
Hoadly, Bishop Benjamin, Ch. II *passim*,
Figs. 13, 24, 25
Hoadly, Dr. Benjamin, 16
Hoadly, John, 16
Hoadly, Mrs., 16, 26-27, *Fig. 16*
Hogarth, William, Ch. II *passim*, 4, 68-
69, 70, 82, 90, 133
The Analysis of Beauty, 16, 23
"Captain Coram," 18-20, 21, 26, *Fig. 17*
"Four Stages of Cruelty," 71
"Harlot's Progress," 20
"Bishop Benjamin Hoadly," Ch. II *pas-
sim*, *Figs. 13, 24, 25*
"Mrs. Hoadly," 16, 26-27, *Fig. 16*
"Marriage à la Mode," 20-23, 68, 83,
Figs. 18-23
"Rake's Progress," 16, 20
"Satan, Sin, and Death," 82-83, *Fig. 61*
Holder, William, 40
Holmes, Sir Charles, 40
Hoppner, John, 39, 60, 63

Hudson (actor), 67
Huntington, Henry E., 39-41, 57, 64, 121

Impressionism, 109
Ipswich, East Suffolk, 30
Isaiah, 47, *Fig. 35*

Jackson, William, 39
Jamaica, 59, 63
Jeremiah, 47, *Fig. 34*
Johnson, Samuel, 35, 45

Kemble, Roger, 44, 67, 77
Knight, Richard Payne, 109

Lacedemonians, 48
Lawrence, Sir Thomas, Ch. V *passim*, 43-
44, 47, 55, 133
"Lady Blessington," 64-65, *Fig. 47*
"Warren Hastings," 64-65, *Fig. 46*
"Pinkie," Ch. V *passim*, *Figs. 43-45*
Le Brun, Charles, 50-51, 52, *Figs. 36-37*
Leonardo da Vinci, 69
linear style, 5
Lorrain, Claude, 12, 94, 96, 130
Loutherbourg, James de, 73
Lyttleton family, 16, *Fig. 15*

Marie Antoinette, Queen, 101-102
Marshall, Ben, 108, *Fig. 83*
Melpomene, 46, 51, *Fig. 38*
Metropolitan Museum, New York, 60
Michelangelo, 47, 48, 49, 52, 53, *Figs.
34-35*
Michelham, Lord, 64
Miller, Thomas, 121
Miller, T. Horrocks, 121
Milton, John, 79-80
Morland, George, 5, 107-108, *Fig. 82*
Mortimer, J. H., 70, 90
Moser, Mary, 32, 38
Moulton, Charles, 59
Moulton, Sarah Goodin Barrett ("Pin-
kie"), Ch. V *passim*, *Figs. 43-45*
Moulton-Barrett, Mrs. Maria Elizabeth,
64

Nash, John, 7, 9, 13, 99
National Gallery, London, 40
Nesbitt (collector), 39
Newey, John, 27
Newton, Richard, 68

Nixon, John, 68
Nollekens, Joseph, 34
Northcote, James, 63

Oakes, Lady, 105

painterly style, 5
Pars, William, 7, *Fig. 5*
Patch, Thomas, 69-71, *Fig. 49*
picturesque, 107-109
Pugin, Augustus Welby, 13

Rembrandt, 3, 48, 52
Reynolds, Sir Joshua, Ch. IV *passim*, 8,
    12, 13, 35, 36, 60, 62, 64, 84, 90, 123, 133
    his theory of art and portraiture, 52
    on Gainsborough, 103
    "Countess of Albemarle," 55, *Fig. 40*
    "Duchess of Hamilton," 55, *Fig. 41*
    "Mrs. Siddons as the Tragic Muse," Ch.
        IV *passim*, 41, 93, *Figs. 33, 42*
    "Lavinia, Countess Spencer," 53, *Fig.
        39*
Richardson, George, 51
Ripa, Cesare, 51, 52, *Fig. 38*
Rialto, Venice, 124, 125, 127
rococo style, 4, 18, 21, 96, 133
Rogers, Samuel, 46, 125
romantic period (in art), 12-13
Romney, George, 5, 60
Romney, Peter, 5, *Fig. 4*
Rosa, Salvator, 12, 99
Rousseau, J. J., 101
Rowlandson, Thomas, Ch. VI *passim*, 5,
    79, 82, 90, *Figs. 48, 50, 54-58*
Ruskin, John, 127, 129
Russell, William, 46

St. Alfege's, Greenwich, 63
Salon, Paris, 120
Sandby, Paul, 73, *Fig. 51*
Schmitz, J., *Fig. 2*
Schroth, Claude, 120
Scudamore, Mrs., 105
Seward, William, 35, 36

Shakespeare, William, 127-128, 129
Sheridan, R. B., 45
Shylock, 128
Siddons, Sarah, Ch. IV *passim*, 67, 75,
    Figs. 33, 42
Sistine Chapel ceiling, 47, *Figs. 34-35*
Smith, J. T., 34
Smith, William, 57
Smith, W. R., 121
Stuart, Gilbert, 55, 60
style (in art), 3-5, Ch. I *passim*
sublime (according to Burke), 86, 99, 107
Syon House, 9, *Figs. 9-12*

Tate Gallery, London, 23, 50
Taylor, G. Watson, 57
Taylor, John, 34
Taylor, Tom, 49
Thomson, James, 128
Titian, 35
Townshend, Lord, 70
Turner, J. M. W., Ch. XI *passim*, 12, 13,
    99, *Figs. 95-106*

Van Dyck, Sir Anthony, 8, 32, 35-36, 38,
    48, 64, 133, *Fig. 29*
Verona, 129
Versailles, 101
Victoria, National Gallery of, Mel-
    bourne, 98, 118
Victoria and Albert Museum, London, 34

Wales, Princess of, 63
Walpole, Horace, 45
Westminster, Duke of, 39, 57
Whitley, William, 30, 35
Wigstead, Henry, 74
Williams, Elizabeth Barrett, 60, 61, 62, 63
Wilson, Richard, Ch. VIII *passim*, 12, 13,
    90, 94, 112, 133, *Figs. 69-75*
Windham, William, 45
Windsor Castle, 15, 18
Woodward, George Moutard, 68
Wyatt, James, 7, 9, 99, *Figs. 7, 8*

Young, John, 35

· 137 ·